IN THE WALNUT GROVE

A CONSIDERATION OF THE PEOPLE ENSLAVED IN AND AROUND FLORISSANT, MISSOURI

Edited by Andrew J. Theising, Ph.D.
for the Florissant Valley Historical Society

Foreword by Carol Daniel

IN THE WALNUT GROVE:
A Consideration of the People Enslaved in and around Florissant, Missouri

Edited by Andrew J. Theising, Ph.D.
Foreword by Carol Daniel

Copyright © 2020 Florissant Valley Historical Society,
P. O. Box 298, Florissant MO 63032
www.florissantvalleyhs.com

DEDICATED TO THE HONOR AND
MEMORY OF THE ENSLAVED PEOPLE
whose hands made the history that we preserve.

TABLE OF CONTENTS

(uncredited sections and articles are by the editor—A.J.T.)

6

This book is a labor of love by several volunteers.
Like any human product, it is imperfect.
Please accept our sincere apologies for any errors or
omissions. While many hands have created this work and
many eyes have reviewed it, there still will be mistakes.
Your patience and understanding, as well as your
corrections and additions, are appreciated.

FVHS

RECOGNIZING THE 1619 PROJECT

In October 2019, *The New York Times* began a landmark series marking the 400th anniversary of British slavery in North America. Nikole Hannah-Jones won a Pulitzer Prize in 2020 for the series. "Our democracy's founding ideals were false when they were written," said Hannah-Jones in an essay. "Black Americans have fought to make them true." While this series marked the 400th anniversary of a specific event in slavery, and may be considered its symbolic start in North America, let us keep in mind that the actual roots of slavery go much deeper— certainly to the 1500s and even to the late 1400s.

The Florissant Valley Historical Society took the opportunity to examine the role of slavery in the Florissant area over that following year through a series of articles and notes in its *Florissant Valley Quarterly* magazine. Those essays are reproduced in this book, which is intended to be a start of a new chapter rather than the conclusion of an old one.

Source: Barrus, Jeff. "Nicole Hannah-Jones Wins Pulitzer Prize for 1619 Project," *Pulitzer Center Update*. 04 May 2020. (https://pulitzercenter. org/blog/nikole-hannah-jones-wins-pulitzer-prize-1619-project)

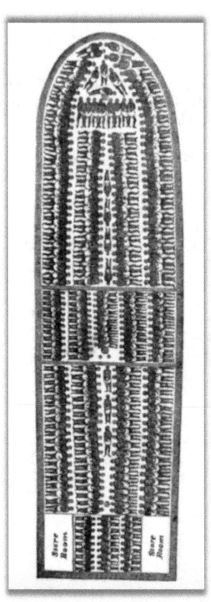

From "Decks of a slave ship," from William O. Blake's History of Slavery and the Slave Trade (1861) Theising image

INTRODUCTION

Florissant's first government was founded just a decade after the American Revolution. In 1786, the Spanish crown established the existing colonial settlement along Coldwater Creek as the City of St. Ferdinand (San Fernando) and shortly thereafter sent Francois Dunegant to be its civil commandant.

Slavery arrived in Florissant in 1796. There were seven enslaved people reported during a Spanish colonial census that year. By the year 1800, as Florissant and the rest of the Louisiana Territory were about to become part of the United States, the number reached 17 and only increased from there.

The earliest census was conducted in 1794-95 in the Spanish territory of Missouri, and it tallied white residents, free Mulattoes, free Negroes, enslaved Mulatto, and enslaved Negro persons. The English colony of Virginia experienced slavery in 1619 and the Spanish colony of Florida experienced slavery as early as 1540 with DeSoto's arrival, so the practice had been in North America for over 250 years by the time of this census. It was present already when the United States was founded. Florissant had no persons of color—free or enslaved—at this time (1). In fact, the whole place had only 157 people.

Florissant did have people who were described as "creole," a dark-skinned ethnic group of mixed heritages in the new world. It comes from an old Latin term that is the root word for "create." Antoine Des Hetres was described by the author Washington Irving as being "a little, swarthy, meager French creole" whom he dubbed "Tonish" in his famous *A Tour on the Prairies*. He was the son of Hyacinthe—a founding citizen of Florissant and the first recorded owner of Taille de Noyer. On the colonial edges of North American empires, people of different backgrounds mixed. In the earliest days of Florissant, it is doubtful that all people looked alike but none were considered Negro. Scharf notes in his history of the county that there were American Indian enslaved people in St. Louis during the colonial period (2).

Thurgood Marshall, attorney in the landmark *Brown vs. Board of Education* decision and later the first African American Supreme Court justice, called the American Constitution "defective" because it openly allowed slavery and skewed the rules of government against these persons of color (3).

Slavery was an abhorrent practice, and just as abhorrent are the racist attitudes and institutional discrimination that have wronged African Americans ever since—depriving our fellow citizens from the safety and security afforded to the white majority.

The purpose of this book is to acknowledge that slavery was a scourge on our society and that its legacy continues in the mistreatment of African Americans to this day. This book acknowledges that enslaved people labored in and around Florissant, that their hands built many of the landmark buildings that we preserve today, and that their history has been neglected. May this book be one step in the direction of healing and reconciliation, and help create safe spaces for much-needed dialogue.

Notes and Sources:
(1) Frazier, Harriet C. *Slavery and Crime in Missouri: 1773-1865*. Jefferson NC: McFarland and Company, 2001. See appendix 2.
(2) Scharf, Thomas. *A History of St. Louis City and County*. Philadelphia: L. H. Everts, 1883. Pg. 1639.
(3) Marshall, Thurgood. *The Bicentennial Speech*. http://thurgoodmarshall. com/the-bicentennial-speech/

FOREWORD

by Carol Daniel

What follows is a history that is often unseen, even though it is all around us. What happened here in St. Louis, here in North County, here in the Florissant area has shaped our world today. It continues to do so.

It is important that we chronicle our common experience. Our local historical societies play an important role in understanding our past, just as journalists work hard to understand the here-and-now. Their goals are the same—to give us information and insight. We have to understand where we come from in order to have a clear vision of where we are and where we're going.

St. Louis is good place with wonderful people. I get to share these stories with you regularly on-air. It is also an imperfect place and we don't have to look very far to find its shortcomings. However, I've learned that if we focus on the inherent goodness in people, we shall see that our community is filled with potential and strength.

This book uncovers an important and painful part of Black History. These pages share first-hand accounts of violence and trauma. Yet, amid this pain are found examples of faith, perseverance, and love. Black History *is* American History. This story is about all of us. And just as we all have to recognize the pain and the legacy, we all have our faith, perseverance, and love to guide us to a better place.

The *Forward through Ferguson* report calls on everyone to welcome and support our continued learning, connection, and dialogue around important issues. This book is one way toward that understanding. With this knowledge, let us work together for a stronger future.

Carol Daniel is an award-winning journalist and host for KMOX Radio in St. Louis. She is an author, and has won recognition for her work in newspapers and television also. She is the president of the Greater St. Louis Association of Black Journalists.

CHAPTER ONE

SLAVERY IN AND AROUND FLORISSANT

A 19ᵗʰ century image of Taille de Noyer. The house had a double porch across the two-story portion in those years. The person standing at left appears to be a worker. FVHS Photo

Slavery at Taille de Noyer
by Andrew Theising

John Mullanphy, Missouri's first millionaire, came to Florissant after the Louisiana Purchase in 1803—though he already owned land in the St. Louis area. He purchased Taille de Noyer (French for "Walnut Grove") in 1805 for $600 in peltry (about $10,000 in today's dollars). He emigrated from Ireland. He followed a path very similar to many Missouri settlers. He first established himself in Maryland (a slavery state), then moved to Kentucky (another slavery state), and then moved north to Missouri (yet another slavery state). He made his millions by cornering the cotton market after the War of 1812, buying all that was available at the port of New Orleans and shipping it at great profit to England, which had been deprived of the commodity during the war and was desperate for it.

John Mullanphy as Slaveholder

The historical record indicates that John Mullanphy was a slaveholder, but scale unknown. In section 5 of his last will and testament, he makes provision for a "Mulatto child called Fanny, now about four years and living with me." He addressed her as property: "I give and bequeath [her] to the Sisters of Charity," the congregation of Catholic religious women who later ran the Mullanphy family's hospital (which is now St. Vincent de Paul Health Center in Bridgeton). He instructed them further: "they are to learn her to read and write and treat her kindly—at the age of eighteen years the said Fanny shall be free absolutely provided that she shall have in the mean time conducted with propriety." He gave further instruction: "And upon her marriage to some decent orderly person, after she shall have become free, I give and bequeath to her the sum of two hundred Dollars" (about $5,300 in today's dollars).

He later added a clarification to his will. "On reading the foregoing last will and testament I perceive that I have made an omission in the fifth article respecting the Mulatto child Fanny." Here he admits his ownership of the family: "I have been induced to make [these arrangements], from commiseration for her destitute situation, as I have sent her mother to a distance for her improper conduct...." Mullanphy made the decision to separate mother and child, then he is here taking ownership of that choice. His motivation for including her in his will, he said, was that he had feelings for the child. "[T]he interest excited in me by the intelligence and smartness of the said Fanny, and from her frequent entertaining and amusing me with her innocent prattle."

Clearly, she had won Mullanphy's affection. He was certain to add, "and in order to rebut and prevent any suspicion or imputation that may exist in consequence of the notice of her in my will, I Solemnly declare before God that she is not my daughter." He made many amendments to his will and wrote this one on or around July 3, 1833. He died on August 29, 1833. The executor of his estate was, in addition to two others, Henry Shaw—the founder and benefactor of what is today the Missouri Botanical Garden.

The term "Mulatto" refers to a parentage of white and Black. It is obvious that Fanny's mother was an enslaved African American. It tragically was common for men in white slaveholding households to rape their enslaved women and father children by them. The children, purely by having a mother of color, were treated as enslaved people instead of the free personage their father was and who instigated the attack. Ethical guidelines make no provision for a consensual affair within power relationships. Today, we would all be familiar with prohibitions against any relationship between a manager and an employee, and it is this same ethical logic that governs relationships then between "owner" and "slave"—which would include the well-known relationship between Thomas Jefferson and Sally Hemings.

In her article "Slave Mothers and White Fathers: Defining Family and Status in Late Colonial Cuba," Karen Y. Morrison writes bluntly about these relationships.

Rape and seduction occupy distinct and unresolved extremes in the historical depictions of these encounters. US African-American historiography has tended to highlight the real violence and mistreatment endured by enslaved Black women.

This portrayal reveals cruel, lustful white masters and overseers who subjected their bondwomen to the dual burdens of chattel labour and sexual abuse. In such situations, female slaves struggled to maintain their dignity but were unable to withstand the brutal onslaught. Family dissolution and personal shame were the results. This historiography has stressed that rarely did the children born to these experiences benefit from any association with a white father. Rather, social conventions and the 'one drop rule' of Black hypodescent ensured that they generally suffered the same denial of their humanity as other enslaved people. (1)

It makes one think about the special risks enslaved women faced (above and beyond the brutality of their enslaved status), and begs the question if Fanny's mother had been raped while in the Mullanphy household. Could the action have been related to the "improper conduct" that was given as the reason for her departure? It is entirely possible that it happened during this time and it may be that Mullanphy knew the father.

Without question, though, Mullanphy profited from slavery. His post-war dealings in the Southern cotton trade, however brief, ensured that fact. He died in 1833. His large family of fifteen children (seven of whom survived to adulthood) married into slaveholding families. There is anecdotal evidence that Mullanphy used indentured servants from Ireland for some of his labor needs—a distinct practice that was parallel to slavery.

Taille de Noyer had been given as a wedding gift in 1817 to his daughter Jane and her husband Charles Chambers. In a letter from May 27, 1818, not long after receiving Taille de Noyer, Jane Chambers described it as "our plantation." Her use of that term is not supported fully by the evidence from a technical point of view. It is unclear how much surrounding land was included in the gift, but Mullanphy owned a considerable amount of it—likely an entire 640-acre "section," or an entire square mile. Chambers himself controlled upwards of 3,000 acres in the area according to Irene Sanford Smith. (2) According to Pitzman's 1878 Atlas, it appears the 1817 gift may have been between 250 and 300 acres. However, after Mullanphy's death, his holdings were divided among his children and it is difficult to discern what land his daughter Jane Chambers held in 1817 vs. 1833.

Charles Chambers as Slaveholder

Charles Chambers was born in Ireland and settled first in New York. He was listed as a slaveholder in the 1850 and 1860 Slavery Censuses. According to the 1850 Slavery Census, Chambers enslaved nine adult and eight children age 10 and under at his location in District 82 of St. Louis—presumably Taille de Noyer. Given the number of children involved, it may be that the total number represents one or two families of enslaved people. Taille de Noyer was the family's country estate and there was also a city home in Ward 3 of St. Louis. Here, Chambers is recorded to have one enslaved person, a 13-year old boy. Likely, Chambers was accompanied by a number of bondspeople as he went between his homes or groups of them would travel where the need was greatest.

His son John Mullanphy Chambers (1822-1861), at age 38, enslaved eight people in 1860—four adults and four children, living in two dwellings. His other son Bartholomew Maziere Chambers (1836-1915), then just 24 years old, enslaved ten—five adults and five children in a single house. Though part of the Chambers family, these men had lands separate from Taille de Noyer. (3) It may be that Charles Chambers gave them both land and enslaved people at a particular point in life. Son Maziere (he went by his middle name) and his wife Marie Walsh lived at "Dunmore," located at Chambers Road and West Florissant Avenue. (4) It had been a gift from Jane Chambers in 1865.

Though the location is a minor detail, it may suggest the type of work enslaved people did for Charles Chambers. It could mean that the enslaved likely did household work rather than field work—not that the nature of the work makes it any less demeaning or cruel. The idea of Chambers having household help rather than field labor may be explained by a letter from Thomas Biddle, who married another Mullanphy daughter (Ann) and who lived in a city house just north of today's Downtown St. Louis.

Biddle was from Philadelphia—where slavery was on the way out—and was also from a family of wealth and power. His father was a military man and leader in Pennsylvania, his brother Nicholas was a prominent banker, his brother John became an early mayor of Detroit, and other brothers were military officers. He wrote in 1826 that "no servants were to be had" in St. Louis, presumably a difference between St. Louis and Philadelphia. Instead, enslaved persons were purchased. He noted that they were "provoking and expensive" and that "a pair of good slaves cost about $750." (5) That's about $17,000 in today's dollars.

Biddle's letter indicates a need for household servants (something he would have been accustomed to as part of Philadelphia's elite) and a desire to hire them for wages if possible. Slavery may have prevented that line of work from developing in St. Louis. In the case of Charles Chambers, he also had the want of household servants and purchased enslaved persons to fulfill that need. Taille de Noyer was a working farm, but farm labor would have been plentiful in and around Florissant.

There are few details of enslaved life at Taille de Noyer. We know that there were marriages among the enslaved people at Taille de Noyer that were held at St. Ferdinand's Church. We also know that the workers would have mingled at church services (seated apart from the white parishioners). We know that they lived in family units, though helpless to try and keep that family together. We can even surmise that the enslaved workers of one household group (e.g., the Chambers) would have mingled with the enslaved workers of related households (e.g., the Grahams).

The historic home still stands, now preserved for a new generation to see. The back stairs of the old house show the wear of two centuries. The old hardwood treads are worn smooth and dipped in the middle. Let us remember that some of the feet on those steps did not walk there by choice, that some of the hands on the handrail were being summoned for service. It is a magnificent old house that accommodated two very different realities.

The Enslaved People of Charles Chambers, Unnamed (6)

Adults:	Children (up to 21)	
Woman, 63	Girl, 20	Boy, 13
Woman, 50	Girl, 15	Boy, 12
Woman, 35	Girl, 4	Boy, 11
Man, 60	Girl, 2	Boy, 9
Man, 44	Boy, 21	Boy, 8
Man, 44	Boy, 19	Boy, 7
Man, 40	Boy, 18	
Man, 40	Boy, 17	

Notes and Sources not noted in-text:
1. Morrison, Karen Y. "Slave Mothers and White Fathers: Defining Family and Status in Late Colonial Cuba," *Slavery and Abolition.* Feb 2010, 31:1, 29-55.
2. Smith, Irene Sanford. *Ferguson: A City and Its People.* St. Louis: Ferguson Historical Society, 1976., p. 123. Regarding Jane Chambers 1818 letter, see *Florissant Valley Quarterly* Vol. 7, No. 4, Oct. 1990. pg. 1.
3. See the 1860 Slavery Census for St. Ferdinand Township, pp. 7, 9.
4. Smith, Irene Sanford. *Ferguson: A City and Its People.* St. Louis: Ferguson Historical Society, 1976, p. 123.
5. Wainwright, Nicholas B. "The Life and Death of Major Thomas Biddle," *The Pennsylvania Magazine of History and Biography*, Vol. 104, No. 3 (Jul 1980), pp. 326-344; p. 333.
6. The estate papers of Charles Chambers, case #6112. St. Louis County Probate Records. *Ancestry.com*

Mullanphy's will was published in 1837 and can be found online through Notre Dame's Hesburgh Library website.

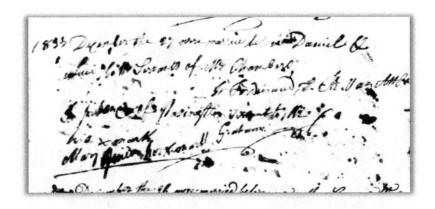

Marriage record from St. Ferdinand's Church, December 27, 1833. Marriage between Daniel and Luci, who were "servants of Mr. Chambers." The marriage was witnessed by "a servant of Mr. Graham," whose name appears to be Washington, and by another who appears to be Mary Queen. The Queen name was associated with the enslaved people at St. Stanislaus, and Mary Queen's burial in 1897 is recorded in the Saint Ferdinand Cemetery record. The record appears to read: "1833 December the 27 were married before me Daniel & Luci, both servants of Mr. Chambers,, St. Ferdinand, Fr. Van Assche, In presence of Washington(?), Servant to Mr. Graham, his (X) mark, Mary Queen, her (X) mark."

Hazelwood Farm's mansion, about 1950s. It was demolished in the early 1960s.
Newspapers.com

The Plantations of the Florissant Valley
by Andrew Theising

The term "plantation" is complicated to define and its social, economic, and political interpretation have shifted. Adrian Graves makes a strong effort to define it in his work (Palgrave 2016). The meanings are varied across time and space. For purposes of this essay, let's focus on three key themes of Graves's definition: a plantation usually cultivates a single crop, does so with involuntary or forced labor, and is often tied to an industrial purpose (e.g., tobacco for a cigar manufacturer) (1). The term generally is associated with size—in this case, acreage and labor force.

Colin Palmer (2) provides structure to the definition. To achieve "planter" status (and therefore run a "plantation"), one would have to enslave greater than 20 persons and cultivate greater than 300 acres. This was uncommon, and those who achieved it felt a degree of social standing and superiority (among other feelings of superiority explicit in slavery).

The sprawling Southern plantation that may come to mind in the antebellum years, then, was a rather atypical experience for slavery. Though they were real places and their conditions were oppressive, this term applied to only the top 12% of slaveholders. Nearly half of those plantations had 20 to 30 enslaved people on them and only the top 5% had 100 or greater enslaved people. Using Palmer's data, we can calculate that in 1860 the average slave-owner enslaved 10 people.

The majority of slaveholders were small rural or semi-rural farmers who had operations on fewer than 300 acres. In the Florissant Valley, there were two major agricultural operations that would qualify as plantations.

Hazelwood Farm

The first was Richard Graham's estate called Hazelwood. Graham and his descendants were the largest slaveholders in the township. Malcolm Graham in the 1860 census recorded 17 enslaved people. An additional 39 are recorded simply under the name "Graham." This would have given the Hazelwood estate "plantation" status and its 640 acres clearly were being worked by enslaved labor—even if the land itself was divided among heirs after Richard Graham's death in 1857.

Graham wrote of the cholera outbreak in 1833. "The cholera made its appearance," he said, "and was followed by the congestive fever which took off sixteen of my Negroes.... It has shattered me a good deal...and I have not as yet recovered from the shock of melancholy feelings in seeing so many human beings dying around me, and looking up to me as their only hope in their despair and their agonies." [speaking of more than just his enslaved people]. (3)

Graham's daughter married General Daniel Marsh Frost, an officer of the Union Army when the Civil War began, but who changed his allegiance to the Confederacy, and then fled both armies by going to Mexico, then Cuba, then Canada with his family for the duration. He and his descendants owned and operated Hazelwood. He returned to the United States in late 1865 and returned to Hazelwood. He died there in 1900.

Today, the land is an industrial park and part of the Boeing complex. There are no remnants of the house or reminders of the people who worked there.

The enslaved people, by name, at Hazelwood at the time of Richard Graham's death in 1857, from his St. Louis County Probate Court records (case #5041), are as follows:

Old John, 80	Anderson, 6 mo	Sarah, 18
Old Bill, 75	Gabe, 10	Martha Anne, 13
Big John, 50	Pete, 8	Eliza, 13
Isaac, 45	John, 18	Matilda, 13
Dave, 32	Ben, 8	Maria, 11
William, 22	Edward, 2 ½	Mimy, 9
Antrim, 32	Lazarus, 4	Alice, 7
Dick, 22	Washington, 2	Jeannette, 2
Jim, 15	Minny, 42	Harriet, 6
George, 11	Kitty, 40	Hester, 5
Bob, 6	Betsy, 65	Amy, 4
Noah, 3	Mary Anne, 30	Mary, 1
Henry, 2	Hester, 28	Betsy, 12
Jerry, 6 mo	Caroline, 34	

Jennings Estate

The second major slaveholder was the family of James Jennings, who came to the area from Virginia in 1839 and brought 40 enslaved people with him. He died in 1855 and the 1860 Slavery Census indicates that the enslaved people were transferred to his wife, Ann B. (Montague) Jennings, and among some of his seven children.) (4) The 1860 Slavery Census identifies 21 enslaved people among three Jennings Family members, including one man astonishingly listed as 100 years old (as well as a woman of 90). Fourteen of the 21 were old enough to have been among the original 40 that came in 1839.

His sprawling estate (which did not seem to have a distinct name) later was bisected by the St. Louis, Kansas City, and Northern Railroad (later the Wabash Railroad), which established "Jennings Station" on the site. The road leading to it bore that name and the surrounding community today is incorporated as the City of Jennings. It is difficult to find the total acreage in historical records, but the 1878 Atlas shows the family still controlled two large portions of the estate at that time, totaling about 250 acres—likely a fraction of what it once was.

A 1951 newspaper article said that Jennings purchased 3,000 acres for $15 in gold when he arrived. His mansion stood on what is now the intersection of Hord and Blewett Avenues. (A plaque marks the location today.) He raised hay that was sold in St. Louis (a single crop that supported the feed market). (5)

The enslaved people for Jennings built a three-story 23-room mansion. It was destroyed by fire in 1923, after serving as the St. Louis Seminary for Young Women. His descendants were named Switzer, McLaran, and Wortley—all streets names in the area. (6)

The enslaved people of the Jennings Estate, by name, from James Jennings's Probate Court record in 1855, (7) follow. Of note, the enslaved person "Fanny, 26" would be the same name and age as the "Fanny" mentioned in John Mullanphy's will in 1833. There is no way to know if this was the same person, but would suggest a tragic outcome if that were the case.

The enslaved people of James Jennings (Probate case #4554):

Ralph, age 57	**Cruel, 43**	**Titus, 62**
Randolph, 45	**Washington, 20**	**Isaac, 49**
Joe, 31	**Marsett, 27**	**Frank, 85**
Ephraim, 30	**Moses, 2**	**Martha, 42**
Jane, 40	**Susan, 12**	**Lucy Ann, 9**
Aggy, 40	**Louisa, 9**	**Sally, 44**
Jack, 48	**Albert, 6**	**Edward, 9**
Isham, 46	**John, 5**	**Eda, 6 mos.**
Jeffry, 12	**Tom, 26**	**Fanny, 26**

The Jennings mansion, built with enslaved labor, shown here c. 1891 when it was the St. Louis Seminary for Women. With permission of the State Historical Society of Missouri, (SHSMO).

Other "Plantations"

Auguste and Pierre Chouteau

Father Gilbert Garraghan, S.J., notes in his 1923 St. Ferdinand history that two members of St. Louis's founding family, Pierre Chouteau and Auguste Chouteau, had "plantations" near Florissant and these lands were located in the area served by St. Ferdinand's Church. (8) A burial record from 1803 is noted for Francois Congeau, "a negro of ninety years," enslaved by Pierre Chouteau, who was interred on the estate by one of the parish priests. In fact, Garraghan identifies a newspaper account stating that Pierre Chouteau had a trading post on Rue St. Francois for 25 years beginning in 1784. The building was later occupied by Mary Aubuchon as a residence and was torn down in 1911. (9)

Auguste Chouteau, descended from the founding family (and the wealthiest) of St. Louis, enslaved at least 30 people. In St. Louis's early years, about half of the enslaved population were American Indians. Spanish colonial leaders abolished *Indian* slavery in the 1770s, but St. Louis slaveholders ignored the decree and the authorities did not enforce it. (10) Chouteau's plantation was in the Bonfils area of what is today Bridgeton MO.

The Missouri Supreme Court abolished Indian slavery in the case *Marguerite v. Pierre Chouteau Sr.* (1834). Though the Missouri Supreme Court decided the case in 1834, the case started in 1825—the time established that Pierre Chouteau had operations near Florissant. There is no clear indication that this case was ever tied to Florissant, though. (11)

It is difficult to determine exactly which Chouteaus were the landowners in St. Ferdinand Township, since each generation named their offspring after the others. The founder of St. Louis was Auguste Chouteau (1749-1829), and he had a brother Jean Pierre, who was known as Pierre Chouteau Sr. (1758-1849). Pierre Sr. had sons Auguste (1736-1838) and Pierre (1789-1865). Auguste, the founder, had a son Auguste (1786-1833). Any or all of these Augustes and Pierres could have owned or inherited these lands in St. Ferdinand Township over time. However, both of the second-generation men named Auguste died out of state—

so clearly they left the area at some point. They both were young enough that Garraghan's 1803 reference to Pierre and Auguste Chouteau in St. Ferdinand's Church records must have applied to the first generation men.

Pierre Chouteau Sr. and his son Pierre both seem to have stayed in St. Louis for the balance of their lives. Garraghan goes to great length to explain that the Chouteaus mentioned in early letters from St. Ferdinand's pastor (Auguste and Pierre) were the sons of Pierre Sr. (12)   Therefore, it appears that both first and second generation Chouteaus were active in St. Ferdinand Township.

Ruins of the old Chouteau manse at Bonfils (Bridgeton), 1871. Two generations of the city's founding family owned land in St. Ferdinand Township. Library of Congress

William and Thomas Gardner

The Gardner Family owned the land along the Maline Creek near Jennings Station Road and Hall's Ferry (in the area that is Moline Acres today). According to Linda Schmerber's history of Jennings, the Gardner Family (William and Thomas) may have been the largest slaveholder in the Florissant Valley—jointly enslaving 47 people. They purchased large tracts of the Jennings Estate (and perhaps the enslaved people associated with the land).

They both are listed in the 1850 Slavery Census but only Thomas is listed in 1860, enslaving eight adults and three children. William died in 1859 and his enslaved people were sold. Thomas's land holdings are found on Pitzman's 1878 Atlas. (13) Families moved to Missouri and brought enslaved people with them.

Notes for this Section:
1. Graves, Adrian. "Plantations," *The New Palgrave Dictionary of Economics*. London: Palgrave-MacMillan, 2016. https://link.springer.com/referenceworkentry/10.1057%2F978-1-349-95121-5_1656-1
2. Palmer, Colin. *Passageways: An Interpretive History of Black America.* New York: Cengage, 1998.
3. Garraghan, Gilbert, S.J. *St. Ferdinand de Florissant.* Chicago: Loyola University Press, 1923.
4. "A Brief History of Jennings," *Jennings.* https://greaternorth countychamber.com/jennings/
5. "Jennings Receives Portrait of Man Who Gave It Name," *St. Louis Post-Dispatch.* 23 Oct 1951, p. 12.
6. "Jennings," *St. Louis Post-Dispatch*, 17 Mar 2019, B4.
7. Schmerber, Linda Ciolek. *Jennings: The Man, the City, and Its People.* St. Louis: Jennings Historical Society, 2011. Pg. 10.
8. Garraghan, 56
9. Garraghan gives the source as a *St. Louis Republic* article, 05 May 1911.
10. O'Neil, Tim. "A Look Back," *St. Louis Post-Dispatch* 17 May 2014.
11. See the case *Marguerite vs. Pierre Chouteau Sr.* in the Washington University Archives. http://repository.wustl.edu/ concern/texts/b2773w92s Marguerite v. Pierre Chouteau Sr.
12. See Garraghan pp. 175-176. See also Foley, W. E. and C. D. Rice, *The First Chouteaus: River Barons of Early St. Louis* (Chicago: University of Illinois Press, 1983) and Cunningham, M. B. and J. C. Blythe, *The Founding Family of St. Louis* (St. Louis: Midwest Technical Publishing, 1977).
13. Schmerber, 11

The editor is grateful to researcher Carol Kane of Historic Florissant Inc. for explaining the details of the Bonfils estate.

Below: Cover page of "Petition for the Sale of Slaves" of the William Gardner estate. The handwritten note on the left half indicates specific instructions: "Sell woman and child for not less than $500, Henry not less than $1000 for cash, private. If not sold private then sell on public, give five days notice at court house door between 10 and 2." Images from William Gardner estate #4937, St. Louis County Probate Court records. Ancestry.com

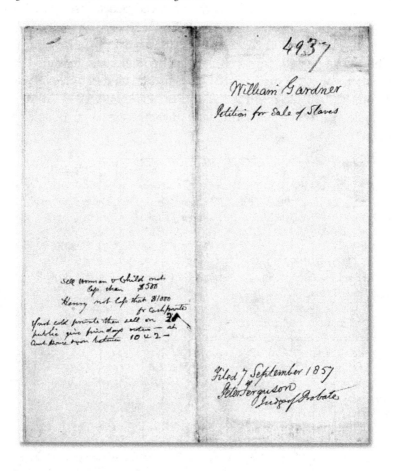

Next page: Though difficult to read, this is an 1859 property tax bill for the estate of William Gardner. The column of lines at the center, near the seal, lists the categories of personal property for taxation. These taxable items include carriages, furniture, libraries, gold and silver plate, and—line five—slaves. This bill was for land tax only. Ancestry.com

To CITY OF ST. LOUIS, Tax for 1859.

Mr. Wm. Gardner

Rest.	Block or Survey.	Frot.	Depth.	Wm. Assess.	L'd.	Bl'k.	State.	DESCRIPTION.		TOTAL VALUE.
							RATE.	ADD'N.	CITY.	DOLLARS. CENTS.

Campbell Cnt's. Hawkins Addn. 12

	DOLLARS.	CENTS.
Valuation 1st........	$4,415	75
Improvements........		
Pers'nal Property....		
Total Value.........	4,415	75
General Tax.........	44	15
Harbor Tax..........	2	24
Sewer Tax...........	4	41
Officers............		
Total of Each.......	50	75

Thos. Laymor
Wm. Patton Dep'y. Collector of
Wards

St. Louis, Octr. 19th 1859. Rec'd Pay't.

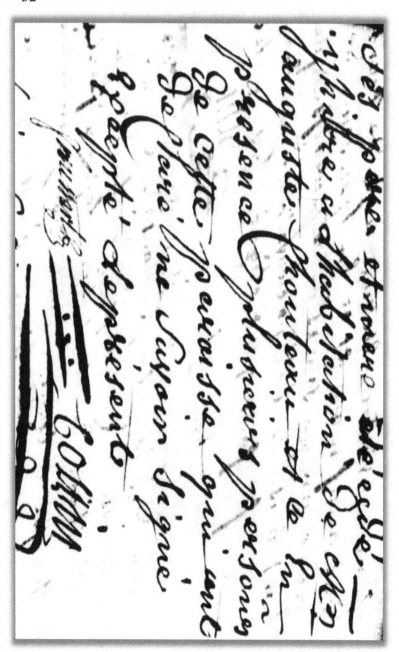

Above: A child's death entry in St. Ferdinand's Church records from 1811, referencing in French "the residence of Mr. Auguste Chouteau." Ancestry.com

An Appeal for Freedom, 1833

This stunning archival record from Slavery, History, Memory, and Reconciliation (SHMR) Research Coordinator Kelly Schmidt's work for the Jesuits, also quoted in the Reynolds book on page 93, shows one man's plea for liberty. **Thomas Brown** requested permission from a Jesuit Superior to purchase freedom for him and his wife. His request was denied.

St. Louis University, October 21, 1833

The humble address of Thomas Brown, a man of colour, most submissively [shows] that he and his wife are very poorly treated by Rev. Father Verhagen, President of the University of St. Louis who is my present master. I have been a faithful servant in the Society going on 38 years, [and] my wife Molly has been born [and] raised in the Society, she is now about 53 years of age.

Now we have not a place to lay our heads in our old age after all our service. We live at present in [a] rotten [log] house, so old and decayed that at every blast of wind we are afraid of our lives and such as it is, it belongs to one of the neighbours.

All the rest of the slaves are pretty well fixed and Father Verhagen wants me and my wife to live on the loft of one of the outhouses where there is no fire place nor any way to warm us during the winter, and your Reverence knows it is cold enough here. I have not a doubt but cold will kill both me and my wife here. To prevent the evil, I am willing to buy myself [and] wife free if you accept of 100 dollars. 50 dollars I can pay down in cash, the rest as soon as I possibly can.

[Reverend] Father, consider this is as much as I can raise [and] as much as our old bones are worth. Have pity on us, let us go free for one hundred dollars or else we will surely perish with the cold.

Oh! [Reverend] Father hear my petition, be pleased to take my case into consideration and I will pray for you while I live.

I impatiently remain [your] Reverence's most humble and obedient servant,

Thomas Brown
A coloured man

N.B. please to direct your letter to Patrick Walsh, Justice of Peace in St. Louis, to be [forwarded] to me at the College.

Note: $100 in 1833 is about $2,700 today. To see the letter, view Ms. Schmidt's research presentation video at shmr.jesuits.org online.

Source: Schmidt's 08 Jun 2018 presentation is recorded at: <https://www.youtube. com/watch?v=ALPUZ9vLnP0> and documentation is at <https://www.jesuits. org/our-work/shmr/updates/> (as of this writing.)

"No Good Masters"

A Review of and Excerpts from William W. Brown's *Narrative*
by Andrew Theising

These were the words of William Wells Brown (1814-1884), an enslaved youth who had bounced around among several overseers in his years of bondage here (1817-1834). He concluded from his experience that there were no good slaveholders and provides ample evidence in his 1847 memoir. "I cannot find a good master in the whole city of St. Louis," he said, "because there are no good masters in the state." (Brown 63-64)

Many today know the name Frederick Douglass—a man born into slavery, who escaped to claim his freedom, and spent his life advocating for abolitionism and civil rights. He was a persuasive speaker and writer. He was vaulted to prominence through his best-selling memoir *Narrative of the Life of Frederick Douglass, An American Slave* in 1845. Under this immense shadow, Brown wrote his own memoir in 1847, *Narrative of William W. Brown, a Fugitive Slave, Written by Himself.* Both books were well received by American and European audiences.

Dr. John Young enslaved the young Brown and the boy's mother, and brought them both from Lexington, Kentucky, to what Brown describes as St. Charles (but today is Warren County). John Young purchased a large expanse of land there, on which he platted the town of Marthasville in 1817. Young did what many other slaveholders often did—rented out the labors of his enslaved people. In practice, enslaved people were hired out much in the same way that today's employers would engage a temporary help firm.

Brown's labor was rented to several people, but of interest here is his time with William Walker. (1) Brown does not give a precise location of William Walker's farm, but he does identify neighbors in his narrative. One of those neighbors was Dr. Bernard Gaines Farrar, who may have been the earliest physician in St. Louis (Brown 88). Farrar's family owned considerable land in St. Ferdinand Township (and enslaved many people). The Farrar Estate included the northeast corner of Chambers Road and West Florissant Avenue. (The Chambers family, according to the Pitzman Atlas, owned the other three corners.) The 1830 Census for St. Ferdinand Township shows

William Walker's name just three lines above Dr. Farrar's. (2, 3)

This places the most notorious part of Brown's book in St. Ferdinand Township. William Walker was a slave-trader who worked a circuit from central Missouri down to the slave-markets of New Orleans, making stops along the way on the Ohio and Mississippi Rivers. He would inquire with slaveholders to see if they had an enslaved person they wanted to sell off downriver. This is exactly the type of person who would have engaged John Mullanphy when he sold Fanny's mother for her "improper conduct." Quite simply, Walker was an evil man with no moral compass. Three stories relayed by Brown illustrate as much.

Brown was forced to work for Walker, and found himself having to facilitate the punishment and enslavement of his fellow African Americans. It was agonizing for him and he knew that if he did not cooperate, he was witnessing his own fate.

On the sexual abuse of enslaved people:

[Walker] had no family, but made a housekeeper of one of his female slaves. Poor Cynthia! I knew her well. She was a quadroon, and one of the most beautiful women I ever saw. She was a native of St. Louis, and bore an irreproachable character for virtue and propriety of conduct. Mr. Walker bought her for the New Orleans market, and took her down with him on one of the trips that I made with him. ...On the first night that we were on board the steamboat, he directed me to put her into a stateroom he had provided for her, apart from the other slaves. I had seen too much of the workings of slavery not to know what this meant. I accordingly [watched and listened].

I heard him make his base offers, and her reject them. He told her that if she would accept his vile proposals, he would take her back with him to St. Louis and establish her as his housekeeper on his farm. But if she persisted in rejecting them, he would sell her as a field hand on the worst plantation on the river.

The next morning, poor Cynthia told me what had passed and bewailed her sad fate with floods of tears.... He took her back to St. Louis, established her as his mistress and housekeeper at his farm, [and fathered four] children by her. [Before Walker later married a white woman, he] sold poor Cynthia and her four children into hopeless bondage! (Brown 45-46)

On the separation of families:

[Walker] bought a number of slaves as he passed the different farms and villages [coming from Jefferson City]. After getting twenty-two or twenty-three men and women, we arrived at St. Charles. Here he purchased a woman who had a child in her arms, appearing to be four or five weeks old. [With no option for other transportation], we started for St. Louis by land. Mr. Walker had purchased two horses. He rode one and I the other. The slaves were chained together.... Soon after we left St. Charles the young child grew very cross and kept up a noise during the greater part of the day. Mr. Walker complained of the crying several times, and told the mother to stop the child's d___d noise, or he would. The mother tried to keep the child from crying but could not.

We put up at night with an acquaintance of Mr. Walker, and in the morning, just as we were about to start, the child again commenced crying. Walker stepped up to her, and told her to give the child to him. The mother tremblingly obeyed. He took the child by one arm, as you would a cat by the leg, walked into the house and said to the lady, "Madam, I will make you a present of this little [Negro]; it keeps such a noise that I can't bear it." "Thank you, sir," said the lady. The mother, as soon as she saw that her child was to be left, ran up to Mr. Walker, and falling upon her knees, begged him to let her have her child. She clung around his legs and cried, "Oh my child! My child! Master do let me have my child! Oh do, do, do! I will stop its crying if you will only let me have it again."

...After the woman's child had been given away, Mr. Walker commanded her to return into the ranks with the other slaves. Women who had children were not chained, but those that had none were. As soon as her child was disposed of she was chained in the gang. (Brown 47-50)

On whipping and punishment:

> *Mr. Walker, though not a good master, had not flogged a slave since I had been with him, though he had threatened me. The slaves were kept in the pen [while traveling the circuit at Vicksburg] and he always put up at the best hotel [and kept good wine]...for the accommodation of those who called to negotiate with him for the purchase of slaves. ...I accidentally filled some of the glasses too full [and the purchasers] spilled wine on their clothes. Mr. Walker apologized [...and...] said he would attend to me. The next morning he gave me a note to carry to the jailer, and a dollar in money to give him. I suspected that all was not right, so I went [to the landing and met a sailor, asking] if he would be so kind as to read the note for me. "...This is a note to have you whipped, and says that you have a dollar to pay for it." ...It is true that in most slave-holding cities, when a gentleman wishes his servants whipped, he can send him to the jail and have it done. (4) (Brown 52-57)*

> *[Before entering Mr. Walker's employ, Brown was rented to the Missouri Hotel, working for a Mr. Colburn there.] Mr. Colburn was very abusive, not only to the servants but to his wife also, who was an excellent woman.... Among the slaves employed at the hotel was one by the name of Aaron, who belonged to Mr. John F. Darby. (5) Aaron was the knife-cleaner. One day, one of the knives was put on the table not as clean as it might have been. Mr. Colburn, for this offence, tied Aaron up in the wood-house, and gave him over fifty lashes on the bare back with a cow-hide, after which he made me wash him down with rum. This seemed to put him into more agony than the whipping.*

> *After being untied, he went home to his master and complained of the treatment he had received. Mr. Darby would give no heed to anything he had to say, but sent him directly back. Colburn, learning that he had been to his master with complaints, tied him up again, and gave him a more severe whipping than before. The poor fellow's back was literally cut to pieces; so much so that he was not able to work for ten or twelve days. (Brown 23-24)*

Brown's tome documents the horrid behavior of a slave-trader in St. Ferdinand Township, but also the indifference that slaveholders (and the users of enslaved labor) showed. Also of interest in Brown's book is a brief time when he was rented to Elijah Lovejoy, the famous newspaper publisher who died in Alton for the cause of abolitionism and free press. At the time Brown worked for Lovejoy (and his paper *The St. Louis Times*), the editor had not developed fully his passion for abolitionism (shown in his subsequent paper *The St. Louis* [and later *Alton*] *Observer*).

Brown makes an important moral argument on which this section shall end. We may be quick to revile the slave-trader like William Walker, who would rape and abuse the human beings in his charge, but "who is it, I ask, that supplies them with the human beings that they are tearing asunder?" It is those who participate in it and are "found among all classes, from [famous Missouri Senator] Thomas Hart Benton down to the lowest political demagogue who may be able to purchase a woman for the purpose of raising stock, and from the doctor of divinity down to the most humble lay member in the church." (Brown 82) While the stories of some are especially vile, it was the everyday people in places like Florissant that enabled them.

Brown wrote the popular novel *Clotel* in 1853, a fictionalized account of the children Thomas Jefferson fathered with the woman he enslaved, Sally Hemings. Because of this work, Brown is considered the first African American novelist.

Above: an ad for the Missouri Hotel from 1829, noting that its new management had selected "the best servants." Newspapers.com

Notes and Sources for this Section:

1. There is an error in the record. The origin of the error is unclear, but it is oft repeated. The man to whom Brown was rented has been called widely "James" Walker. While there was a James Walker in St. Ferdinand Township, biographer and scholar Ezra Greenspan notes that it was actually William Walker who was the notorious slave-trader. (See Greenspan, Ezra. *William Wells Brown: An African American Life*. New York: W. W. Norton, 2014. Pp. 61-62.) This can be verified by examining the court records (see, for example, *Rachel vs. William Walker* in the Washington University archives online— http://repository.wustl. edu/concern/texts/t722h9873).

2. Though he resided in the Township, there is no evidence readily found that William Walker owned the land on which he operated his business. While there were landowners with the last name Walker, there is no evidence that they were related to William. The most significant Walker in the Township was John Kelso Walker, a prominent politician who served as one of the first sheriffs of St. Louis. His estate was on the Halls Ferry Plank Road and he enslaved several people—all of whom were sold upon his death in 1858. See his St. Louis County Probate Records (case number 5324, adjudicated in 1862). For a complete history of the John Kelso Walker family, see White, Emma Siggins. *Genealogy of the Descendants of John Walker of Wigton, Scotland*. Kansas City: Tiernan-Dart, 1902. There is no obvious connection between John Kelso and William. John's son James Walker M.D. lived in the township too.

3. Dr. Farrar's widow, Ann C. Farrar, appears in the slaveholder tables later in this chapter.

4. The digitized copy of the book has a defect in the middle of this story. Apparently, Brown used some kind of deception to send another man to punishment instead of himself—an action he laments and wishes for which he could make amends. The details are unclear. The point of this excerpt is that punishment was meted out for minor offenses, and that public officials (the county jailor) did some of the dirty work for slaveholders.

5. John Fletcher Darby was the fourth Mayor of St. Louis and later elected a Member of Congress. He is associated with "Darby's Hill," which appears in the 1878 Pitzman Atlas as being near the Lucas and Hunt properties between Natural Bridge and St. Charles Rock Road in Central Township. He was one of the signatories on the petition for the incorporation of Florissant (then, St. Ferdinand) in 1857. He was a dear friend of Edward Bates of Florissant, which probably was the connection to the city's incorporation

Primary Source: Brown, William Wells. *Narrative of William W. Brown, An American Slave, Written by Himself*. London: Charles Gilpin, 1849. (available on Google books). The US edition was in 1847. Illustration is the frontispiece.

1860 Census, St. Ferdinand Township, Free Inhabitants Identified as Black or Mulatto

Compiled by Cindy Winkler

Out of 120 pages of census records, approximately 40 people per page, Free Black and Mulatto residents of St. Ferdinand Township, St. Louis County, Missouri, appeared on only seven pages. These entries are summarized, with notes, in the following table.

Name (first last)	Age	Sex	Race	Occupation	Place of Birth	Value of Real/Personal Estate
Sandy Fugit	30	M	B	Farm Hand	MO	500/300
Note: Sandy Fugit is listed within Henry Massey's Household						
Abraham Roder	46	M	B	Farmer	VA	1,000/200
Elizabeth Roder	35	F	B		VA	
Abraham Roder, Jr.	18	M	B		MO	
Charles Roder	16	M	B		MO	
Jack Roder	5	M	B		MO	
Tom Roder	3	M	B		MO	
Mary Roder	14	F	B		MO	
Eliza Roder	9	F	B		MO	
Sam Roder	1	F	B		MO	
Note: It is marked that Jack, Tom & Eliza attended school over the past year; perhaps, however, it was Jack, Mary and Eliza since they are school aged.						
Burr Powell	51	M	B	Farmer	VA	500 Personal Estate
Note: Mr. Powell appears to have his own dwelling, but perhaps does not own it. Seven men also reside here: Four from Ireland, One from Germany, One from Wales, and one from Missouri.						

Emily Bates	13	F	B	No Occupation	MO	
Note: Emily Bates lives with the William B. Ferguson Family						
Franklin Pope	55	M	B	Servant	KY	
Angeline Pope	57	F	B	Servant	VA	
James Pope	36	M	B	Servant	MO	
Elizabeth Pope	33	F	B	Servant	MO	
Clinton James	40	M	B	Servant	MO	
John James	11	M	B	Servant	MO	Attended School within past year

Jason James	10	M	B	Servant	MO	Attended School within past year
George James	4	M	B	Servant	MO	
Elizabeth James	13	F	B	Servant	MO	Attended School within past year
Franklin Pope	17	M	B	Servant	MO	
John Pope	15	M	B	Servant	MO	
Angeline Hammond	27	F	B	Seamstress	MO	
George Hammond	2	M	B		MO	
Robert Hammond	6/12	M	M		MO	
Melinda Hammond	4	F	B		MO	
Berry Williams	47	M	B	Gardener	GA	
Hannah Williams	48	F	B		VA	
James Williams	24	M	B	Gardener	MO	
Berry Williams, Jr.	20	M	B	Gardener	MO	

1860 Census, St. Ferdinand Township
Enslaved Inhabitants
by Slaveholder Household
June 1860

Compiled by Cindy Winkler

There were 853 enslaved people in the St. Ferdinand Township in 1860. The total population of the township was 4,800, so a substantial percentage of the population was in bondage.

Slaveholder names in *italic* font followed by a (number) refer to the census files located in the galleries on the historical society website, www.florissantvalleyhs.com. These markers correspond with 1870 census records where individuals or families identified as Black or Mulatto live either with or near former slaveholders. This information is also discernable from the 1870 census tables found in the next chapter of this book.

Name of Slaveholder	Number of Enslaved People	Number of Houses for Enslaved	Notes
K. Stent	3	1	
T.G. Adams	1	1	
Benjamin Watkins	1	1	
Rosa Watkins	1	0	
Thomas C. Minnie	1	1	
Stokes Thorp (1)	5	2	
W.L. Larimore	8	3	
Rachael Larimore	8	0	
D.D. St. Vrain	2	2	
Susan St. Vrain	1	0	
Mary St. Vrain	1	0	
Henry Carter	7	2	
Paschal Crow (2)	1	1	
Malena Fugit	3	1	
Elizabeth McClure	1	1	

James Gousollis	3	2	
James Loup	7	2	
A. Alvarez	1	1	
Jessit Alvarez	2	1	
Pascal St. Cyr (3)	2	2	
Dr. Gibson (4)	10	2	
James Bissell (5)	10	2	
Green Larymore	3	1	
John Dyson	11	1	
Frederick Price (6)	3	1	*Number Fugitives from the State: 1*
James B. Redman (7)	2	1	
Samuel Henley	3	1	*"Samuel Durkin"? born 1820, Male, Black, is one of the 3*
Chas Lewis	2	2	
W.S. Veirs	6	2	
Frederick Hyatt (8)	10	3	
Frederick St. Cine	2	1	*Number Fugitives from the State: 1*
Jesuit College	28	3	*Oldest man is 90 / Born 1770*
Mary Letcher	1	0	*14-year-old Black male*
Augustus Archambault	1	0	*21-year-old Mulatto male*
John A. Smith	1	0	*14-year-old Black male*
John Plant	6	2	
Frederick Hyatt (again)	1	3	
Elizabeth Hyatt (10)	8		
Jacob Veale (11)	1	0	*37-year-old Black male*
John Ferguson	1	1	
Benj Buel	1	0	*9-year-old Black female*
Michael Cerre Estate (12)	1	1	*One man named Frank per Probate Inventory*
W.W. Evans	12	2	

Joseph Patterson	2	1	
Nicholas Douglas (13)	6	1	
John Shackelford	5	2	*Number Manumitted: 2*
Pryor Patterson	5	1	
W.P. Peterson	3	1	
Jas B. Walker, MD (14)	10	3	
W.W. Evans	11	1	
Reuben Musick (15)	12	3	
Elizabeth Tyler	7	2	
Benjamin Douglas	4	1	
Sarah A. Humes (16)	3	1	
William H. Humes	4	1	
Stuart Hall	4	1	
Margaret Fowler	3	1	
James James	1	0	*7-year-old Black male*
Gregwell Overshaw	3	1	
John Hyatt (17)	5	2	
Thomas M. Turnstall	6	2	
Richard Shackelford	6	1	
Mary Harris (18)	6	1	
Durrett Patterson	3	1	
Edward Hall	6	1	
John Massey	5	1	
Franklin Utz (19)	15	2	
T.G. McHatton	8	2	
Mary St. Cyr	1	0	*15-year-old Black female*
Walter B. Morris	18	2	
W.K. Vaughan	1	1	
Robert Martin	8	1	
George Hall	4	1	
George Martin	11	1	
Edward James	1	0	*14-year-old Black male*
George Withington	1	0	*14-year-old Black female*
Nicholas Riddle	2	0	*41-year-old Black male and 16-year-old Black female*
Mary Yosti	10	1	

Graham (20)	39	5	*Fugitives: 5; 24 Black, 15 Mulatto*
Nathaniel Covington	3	1	
Thos Gardner (21)	11	1	
Willis Hord	11	1	
Wm. A. Eads	4	1	
Charles Conoyer	2	1	
Thomas B. Hudson	2	1	
W.Z. Coleman	5	1	
Frank Reyburn (22)	17	2	
Walker	5	1	
Ann C. Farrar (23)	18	3	
D.A. John Farrar	6	1	
Thos January	14	2	
B. Maziere Chambers (24)	10	1	
Joseph H. La Motte	6	1	
Lewis Rose (25)	2	1	
William Leslie Estate	1	0	*37-year-old Mulatto Female*
Hind F. B. Powell	6	1	*5-year-old Black male noted to be "idiotic"*
Nancy Sheppard	9	1	
Thos. G. Settle	1	0	*40-year-old Black Male*
Judge Locklane	2	1	
Evans Locklane	5	--	*Assume with Judge Locklane*
Aubrey Naylor	1	1	
R. Jennings	1	--	*Assume with Aubrey Naylor*
Ann B. Jennings	15	1	*100-year-old Black Male, Manumitted; 35-year-old Black Male, Manumitted, 35-yr-old Black Male, Manumitted, 9-yr-old Black Female, Manumitted*

Dr. John C. Jennings	5	1	
Doctor D. Benton	9	1	
Emily Taylor	1	0	*15-year-old Black male*
Joseph C. Beard	4	1	
Agustus Alvarez	10	1	
Eleanor Clark	7	1	
Saml James	2	0	*19-year-old Black Female and 1-year-old Black Female*
Dr. Julian Bates	3	1	
Mackay Wherry	3	1	
Mary Fugett	2	0	*22 year-old-Black Female and 5-year-old Black Female*
Caroline Brown	1	0	*6-year-old Black Female*
Catha Hance	1	0	*10-year-old Black Female*
Henry Gross	6	1	
Ellen Bush	6	1	
William S. Taylor	12	2	
John James	1	0	*100-year-old Black Male*
J.G. Musick	3	1	
John Bagart	2	1	
Owen Musick	1	0	*13-year-old Black Female*
Antonio Lomraino	2	1	
Alena Berther	5	1	
Andrew Harper	5	1	*Number Manumitted: 24 (Also age of first person listed, so could be a mistake)*
John Chambers	8	2	
Robert F. Logan	1	0	*75-year-old Black Female*

Miss Morris	2	0	*20-year-old Black Female and 1-year-old Black Male*
Benjamin Stephens	4	1	
George Moore	2	1	
Elizabeth Smith	2	1	
Joseph H. Garrett	2	1	
Samuel McClure	1	0	*18-year-old Black Female*
David Thomas (26)	4	1	
R.E. Bland	4	1	
George Robertson	4	1	*1 Fugitive From the State*
Sallie Long	2	1	
Daniel Eaches	10	1	
John Quesenberry	4	2	
George Lackland	4	1	*4 Fugitive From the State (!)*
George Penn	15	3	
Nancy Achausen	5	1	
Rich Jenkins	1	0	*13-year-old Black Female*
Deliah McKelvey	4	1	
Carter Moss	2	1	
James Dawson	3	1	
Erastus Post	7	1	
J.T. Thompson	15	2	
Rebecca Davis	5	1	
Robert Edmons(t)on	15	3	
Will W. Henderson	4	1	
Edw Thomas	3	1	
William Grinalder	5	1	
L. Desruissceaux	10	2	
James C. Edwards	7	1	
Malcolm Graham	17	2	
Lucian M. Mead	4	1	

Prominent Florissant Slaveholders

<u>Augustus Alvarez</u> (1797-1878), son of Eugenio Alvarez who had been a leading citizen during colonial rule. His family lived in Florissant for generations.

<u>August Archambault</u> (1817-1880): trapper, explorer, mountain man. He was associated with John C. Fremont's westward expeditions. Fremont's wife, Jessie Benton Fremont (daughter of Senator Thomas Hart Benton), was keen to speak out on society's injustices.

<u>Julian Bates, M.D.</u> (1833-1902), town physician, one-term mayor, son of U.S. Attorney General Edward Bates. See Lucy Delaney's story later in this book for more on the Bates family.

<u>Francois Dunegant</u>: first civil and military commandant of Florissant in 1786. He owned a plot of land near Bellefontaine containing, presumably, an Indian mound, which he cultivated from 1768 to 1782 (a few years before coming to Florissant). He acquired this from his late wife, Catherine Noise dit Labbe, who had acquired it from her first husband, J. B. Langoumois. This land was transferred to John Mullanphy in 1805. However, when Mullanphy's estate went to court in the 1850s, Catherine Noise's nephew testified that he witnessed enslaved people working the farm back in the day. (See Garraghan 46-47)

<u>Samuel James</u> (1817-1898): descendant of one of the earliest residents; city treasurer and later longtime judge of the St. Louis County Court.

<u>Joseph Roubidoux II</u>: He came to St. Louis from Montreal with his father, Joseph I, who was a very wealthy fur trader. Joseph II obtained 1150 arpents of land around Florissant, which he sold to John Mullanphy in 1806. The St. Ferdinand Church records indicate the burial of "certain slaves" that belonged to Mr. Roubidoux. Joseph III was the founder of St. Joseph MO. (Garraghan 54)

<u>James Castello</u> (d. 1878): Prominent political figure in St. Louis and Colorado. While not listed personally as a slaveholder, he did

serve one term as St. Louis County Sheriff and would have been responsible for jailing and auctioning off enslaved people. He left Florissant, Missouri, and went westward in 1860. He established a hotel in Colorado, served in the territorial legislature, and, in 1872, he founded Florissant, Colorado, named after his favorite Missouri city.

Sheriff's Sale of Runaway Slaves.

NOTICE is hereby given, that on the Ninth day of September, 1856, there was taken up and committed to the common jail of St. Louis county, as a runaway slave, a mulatto man calling himself John Frazier. Said Frazier is about thirty years of age, five feet two inches in height, and weighs about 135 pounds, and had on when committed, striped cotton pants, check shirt, glazed cap, and grey jeans coat. And on the 16th day of September, 1856, there was committed to said jail as a runaway slave, a mulatto man, calling himself David Hagan. He is about twenty-seven years of age, five feet four inches in height; and weighs about 160 pounds; says he belong to John Prichard, of Portland, Kentucky; had on when committed a cotton undershirt, grey pants and a blue drill coat. And on the 13th day of November, 1856, there was committed to said jail, as a runaway slave, a mulatto man calling himself Porter Fox. He is about 26 years of age, five feet six or seven inches in height, and weighs about 145 pounds; had on when committed, a grey cotton coat, white hat, black vest, black pants and check shirt.

The owners of said slaves are hereby required to make application for same for said slaves, and pay all charges incurred on their account, on or before

Monday, the Sixteenth day of March, 1857,

otherwise I will sell the said slaves at public auction, for cash, on said last mentioned day, at the east front door of the Court House, in the city and county of St. Louis, State of Missouri, according to the statute in such cases made and provided.

JAMES CASTELLO, Sheriff.

1857 Advertisement by James Castello, of Florissant, who was the St. Louis County Sheriff. It is tragic that those who sought to escape slavery were captured, rented while imprisoned, and returned to a life of bondage. Newspapers.com

For more on Castello, see "A Tale of Two Florissants," *The Mountain Jackpot News.* https://www.mountainjackpot.com/ 2013/09/20/a-tale-of-two-florissants/

Eliza Nebbit (c. 1811-1889)   Courtesy of the Society of the Sacred Heart

A "Colored Child of the Sacred Heart"

A letter dictated by **Eliza Nebbit**
to Rev. Mother Randall in 1880,
[and reproduced here in dialect as published in 1914]

St. Michael's Plantation

Dear Mother:

It seems as what it is an age since I received de letter you sent me fur to have a mass said fur yore 'tentions and fur to have all de darkies in dese parts to exist at dat holy sacrifice, but I has been so upside down wards fur dese last six weeks dat I ain't had no time to think ob nothing but my pore ole soul, what has had a heap o' sorrow an tribulations, but I wants you to have a good understanding of what for I had not sent you a letter long afore dis present time.

First and foremost I was a waitin' fur dis here Lady what is a settin' in my Cabin now a writin' down all what I tells her to say, cause she knows you and all dem Yankees up in your part of de world and I knowd she was coming up here wid my child, Madam Mary Moran fur to see our ole Archbishop what is stayin' on dis here Convent plantation fur to be took good care of till he gets over dis spell of sickness, dat is why & de wherefore dat you aint done got a letter from Liza long afore now. I hopes dat you has a good understandin' of my 'pology, cause I was riz by dese ladies of de Sacred Heart & I don't want to bring disgrace on dem by bad manners fur Madame Duchesne and Madame Aloysius Hardy was mighty pertiklar when they was raisin' me to show Liza what was right and what was left so I knowd politeness most as well as de white folks and fifty times better dan any of my kin and color.

All de members of dis here colored congregation sends dere bess love an compliments to all you ladies, dey will join in de Mass when our director says it next week; dey has all been invited to exist at de Mass and communicate, maybe I'll go and maybe I'll not go, cause you see I'se in great affliction at dis present time; my legs swelled up like two drums, my feet is so sore I can't put on my shoes. De Father says, Liza, put on a long gown and go to de holy table in yer bare feet, but I said no: I ain't goin to make any show like I was so wirtuous when all de folks knows dat Liza ain't no saint. I ain't going to do no such thing, de Lord 'flicts me and when he thinks dat I'se done suffered enuff den he make de way smooth—but now its all hills and hollows and de pebbles and de sharp bits o' rock in mighty smart—but den de Lord knows how many thorns He put on de briar-bush and it seems like He soon tell me to quit—dat he's tired 'flictin' pore old Liza and wants to give her a rest. I don't say dis to grumble bout His hand what is laid so heavy on me, but to splain de reason dat may prevent me to exist at yore Mass, but de Lord is in my ole Cabin and I kin pray dare fur all you ladies of the Sacred Heart.

My chile looks mighty smart, but I done cried a hogshead o' tears cause she can't be 'suaded to come an' live here quiet at St. Michael's sence she's been Superior she's like a spirit going everywhere. I blames Madam Aloysia Hardy fur givin' des Superiors here in Louisiana dese idays about flittin' from house to house; afre she was come down hare dey was all quiet and contented to stay in de same convent from de beginning to de end of dar days, but she comes and gives im a taste for cars and boats, an since den dey is every one like de moon what is always changin' and a changin'; but I ax de Lord to leave my chile here to me so I can keep an eye after her health—she's so valuable to dis here Society dat she ought to be took double care of; ef I see her cheeks a sinkin' in and her complexion gittin like white wash, I'll keep a jawin' an a grumblin' till dey send her back to dat ar Halifax fur I don't never want agin to see her look like chalk like she used to. I'se taxed wid de Rhumatiz and a heap o' other misfortunes an it 'pears to me like ole Liza won't do uch more in ids world, it seems like her web is most spun—dare ain't much yarn left on de spool an de Lord's pretty nigh settin' His foot again the wheel fur to stop it from whirlin' round any more, so if ye don't hear any more from Liza ye needn't be sprized. Please present my compliments to all you ladies of de Sacred Heart and tell "Howde" to every one of them. I love them all, dey is all locked up in my heart cause de was 'fectionate & 'tentive to my pore sick chile, Mother Moran.

I draw my letter to a close with love

Liza Nebbit

Colored child of the Sacred Heart, first slave what was brought in dis Convent by Mother Duchesne.

The accompanying published notes from 1914 state that Bishop Louis William Valentine DuBourg somehow acquired little Eliza Nebbit along one of his journeys. She was between seven and 12 years old and a "sickly, neglected child." Bishop DuBourg left Eliza with Mother Duchesne about 1821. She stayed in Florissant until 1825, when she went with Mother Eugenie Audé to do the Society's work in Louisiana. (Mother

Audé was one of Mother Duchesne's companions who made that initial trip to Florissant in 1819 to establish the convent.)

Eliza married twice and remained a devoted servant to the Sisters. She lived on the convent grounds and received permission to be buried in the convent cemetery at St. Michael's. Of interest is how she still referred to the convent as "St. Michael's Plantation," decades after the end of the Civil War.

For the last few years, the Society of the Sacred Heart's US-Canada Province has "worked humbly to acknowledge our history with enslavement" by reaching out to descendants of the persons enslaved and working with them toward building racial equity and ending systemic racism. The Province's Committee on Slavery, Accountability and Reconciliation continues to work diligently on "The Mandate:"

> *"To focus on the on-going issue of racism in the world and the Society of the Sacred Heart's participation in the historic sin of slavery. ...we commit ourselves to recover the story of slavery in our early days in this country, to share this historical fact as widely as needed, to assist in the attempt to locate the descendants of enslaved persons who lived on property owned by the Society of the Sacred Heart, and to take appropriate steps to address this painful chapter in our history while also working to help transform on-going racist attitudes and behaviors."*

Notes and Sources:

"Letter of a Colored Child of the Sacred Heart," *Records of the American Catholic Historical Society of Philadelphia.* Philadelphia: Privately published, 1914. Pp. 179-181.

Research by the Society of the Sacred Heart indicates that her parents were Henry Nebit or Nobit, and Jenny Burch. She appears to have had at least one sister, Sarah. One of her marriages, according to Society records, was unhappy. The husband took all of her property and fled. She raised five children in her household, one of whom was her nephew. Segregation laws prevented her from joining the order, which she desired to do. For more, please see "About Eliza 'Liza' Nebbit," at the Society's website: <https://rscj.org/about-eliza-liza-nebbit>. The Slavery, Accountability, and Reconciliation Work is found at: <https://rscj.org/history-enslavement>.

Of note, there is a man named Samuel Nebbit, who died in 1929, buried in Washington Park Cemetery in St. Ferdinand Township.

Above: the famous portraits of **Dred Scott and Harriet Robinson Scott** *that appeared in* Frank Leslie's Illustrated News Paper, *June 27, 1857. Their freedom suit, in a sense, started in St. Ferdinand Township.* SHSMO

St. Ferdinand Township's Connection to the *Dred Scott* Case

by Andrew Theising

John Francis Alexander Sanford (famously misspelled in the Supreme Court case as "Sandford" and oft-repeated) was a very successful business partner of Pierre Chouteau Jr. He was a graduate of West Point and was assigned to St. Louis in 1829, where he eventually connected with Pierre Chouteau Jr. and married into that family. Sometime between 1834 and 1836, he moved his father, Alexander, from Virginia to St. Ferdinand Township, undoubtedly purchasing some of the Pierre Chouteau land around Bonfils. (1)

Alexander Sanford was a pro-slavery Virginian who lived on the St. Ferdinand Township estate purchased for him, which he called "California." (2) John arranged a business enterprise for his father with the Bertholds—also part of Pierre Chouteau's extended family.

About this same time, John's sister Eliza Irene Sanford married an army surgeon who had been stationed for a time at Jefferson Barracks (though it is unclear how they met). Dr. John Emerson enslaved a man who was his body servant or valet—Dred Scott. While in bondage to Dr. Emerson, Dred Scott traveled with him to posts that were in free territory, laying the groundwork for his eventual legal challenge. While stationed at Fort Snelling, Minnesota, Dred met and married Harriet Robinson in a civil ceremony in 1837 or 1838 (an unusual occurrence for enslaved people, but this did not happen in a slavery state). Dr. Emerson somehow acquired Harriet from her owner at Fort Snelling (the record is unclear) and they traveled extensively with Dr. Emerson until 1840, when he ultimately sent them to St. Louis where they were hired out. (3)

Dr. Emerson died unexpectedly in 1843 while stationed in Florida. Dred and Harriet were both still hired out during this time. Irene, Dr. Emerson's widow who considered herself the rightful owner of the Scotts, moved to St. Ferdinand Township to live with her father. She lived here when the Scotts launched their freedom suit. The father's pro-slavery views must have guided Irene's thinking in the case. Her brother, John, managed her affairs and ultimately became the defendant in the suit.

The Scotts were imprisoned during their lawsuit and rented for hire by the Sheriff. They lived this way from March 17, 1848 to March 18, 1857. (4) The sheriff who would have released them on that last day was James Castello of Florissant. (See the section "Prominent Florissant Slaveholders" in Chapter One of this book.)

Dred Scott died of consumption one year after his case was lost and he was released from jail. He died a free man, though. Alexander Sanford had died in 1848, and Irene Sanford moved to Massachusetts in 1850. There, she married Dr. Calvin C. Chaffee—an outspoken abolitionist and member of Congress. Imagine the cries of hypocrisy that erupted when it was discovered that the wife of the abolitionist Congressman was the owner of the most famous enslaved couple in the world! Chaffee wrote a sincere public apology published widely and claimed he did not know of the suit or have influence in it. (5) After all, the case was against his pro-slavery brother-in-law in St. Louis—not his wife. After the Supreme Court case, when ownership was officially determined to be with Irene Sanford Chaffee, Dr. Chaffee deeded Dred and Harriet to Henry Taylor Blow of St. Louis, who gave them their freedom. (Ironically, it was Blow's parents that enslaved Dred Scott first and sold him to Dr. Emerson.)

Frederick Douglass called the Scotts' freedom a victory over slavery—though he wondered aloud frankly if it was motivated by "sympathy with the slave" or was "purely a white man's victory." It was a victory nonetheless, he noted, and he projected that slavery was "doomed to cease out of this otherwise goodly land." (6) Eight years later, he would be proven right.

Harriet continued to live in the area as a free woman until her death in 1876. She was buried away from her husband in the Greenwood Cemetery, just outside St. Ferdinand Township along cemetery row (St. Charles Rock Road).

Notes and Sources for Dred and Harriet Scott Section:
(1) There is only circumstantial evidence to show this. It is clear that the 1840 Census of the township was solicited from north to south based on the order of entries. John's father, Alexander, is found in the 1840 census as being enumerated between Richard Graham (Hazelwood) and the January family (Kinloch), indicating a location somewhere around today's Lambert International Airport. We know that John purchased the land for his father, and we know that he married into Pierre Chouteau's family. Pierre Chouteau

owned plenty of land adjacent to Auguste's estate at Bonfils near today's airport, and so it is reasonable to assume that the father lived on a portion of Chouteau land. Kaufman (see next note) confirms this thinking.

(2) See Kenneth Kaufman, *Dred Scott's Advocate* (University of Missouri Press, 1996) p. 145. See also Lea Vandervelde, *Mrs. Dred Scott: A Life on Slavery's Frontier.* (Oxford University Press, 2009), pp. 362 n42, 378 n42.

(3) and (4) See "Dred Scott," *Historic Missourians* found at https://historic missourians.shsmo.org/historicmissourians/name/s/scottd/

(5) See his letter published in several sources, including *The Liberator* (Boston, MA), 20 Mar 1857, p. 3. Regarding the death of Alexander Sanford, his estate was handled by John F. Darby, mentioned in the "No Goods Masters" article in Chapter One of this book.

(6) Douglass, Frederick. *Two Speeches of Frederick Douglass.* Rochester NY: Dewey, 1857. Page 35.

Below: Title page of the court case, 1857. Note the misspelling of the Sanford name by the court.

A REPORT

OF THE

DECISION OF THE SUPREME COURT

OF

THE UNITED STATES,

AND THE

OPINIONS OF THE JUDGES THEREOF,

IN THE CASE OF

DRED SCOTT

versus

JOHN F. A. SANDFORD.

DECEMBER TERM, 1856.

BY BENJAMIN C. HOWARD,
COUNSELLOR AT LAW AND REPORTER OF THE DECISIONS OF THE SUPREME
COURT OF THE UNITED STATES.

NEW YORK:
D. APPLETON & Co., 346 & 348 BROADWAY.
1857.

THE CASE OF DRED SCOTT. The Springfield *Republican* has a letter from Dr. Chaffee in regard to the connection of his family with this case. We copy the material portion thereof:

'In the case of Dred Scott, the defendant was and is the only person who had or has any power in the matter, and neither myself nor any member of my family were consulted in relation to or ever knew of the existence of that suit till after it was noticed for trial, when we learned it in an accidental way,—and I agree with you, that if I had been possessed of any power or influence in the case, and failed to use it, then I should have been 'guilty of treason to my professions, and a betrayal of the confidence of my constituents.'

But possessed of no power to control—refused all right to influence the course of the defendant in the cause—and all the while feeling and openly expressing the fullest sympathy with Dred Scott and his family, in their efforts to secure their just rights to freedom— no man in this land feels more deeply the intense wrong done, not only them, but the whole people, by the monstrous decision of the majority of the U. S. Supreme Court. And if, in the distribution of the estate, of which this decision affirms these human beings to be part, it appears that I or mine consents to receive the *thirty pieces of silver*, then—and not till then—let the popular judgment, as well as the public press, fix on me the mark of a traitor to my conscience, as well as to the true rights of our common humanity.

I believe that, under the Constitution and laws of this Union, these colored persons have become not only freemen, but citizens, and I stand ready to rally with the rest of the people under the banner which proclaims and promises to vindicate their rights.

I remain, respectfully,

C. C. CHAFFEE.

Springfield, March 14.

Above: Dr. Calvin Chaffee's 1857 public letter apologizing for any perceived role he had in the case Dred Scott vs. Sandford, *and affirming the rights of African Americans to freedom. Newspapers.com*

Below: Sale of Alexander Sanford's enslaved people in 1849: **Solomon, John, Isaac, and Mary** *at center. Signed by John F. A. Sanford at the very bottom— clearly showing the proper spelling of his last name. Ancestry.com*

Below: The 1846 summons that would have been served at Alexander Sanford's St. Ferdinand Township estate for Irene Emerson to appear at the Old Courthouse. It started the long path to the Supreme Court in 1857.   SHSMO

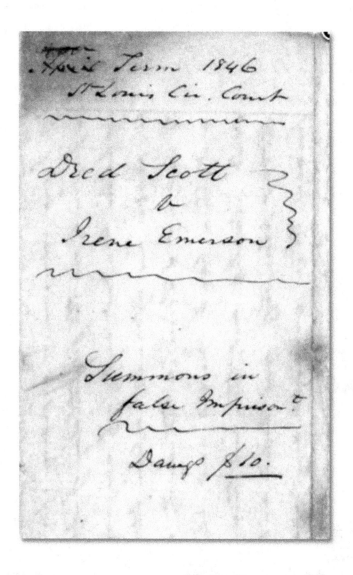

CHAPTER TWO

THE CENTURY
AFTER EMANCIPATION

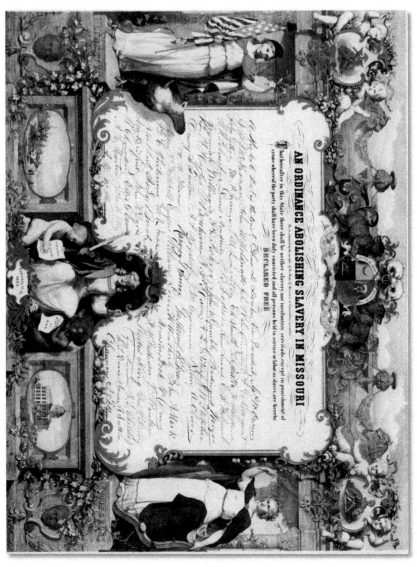

A History of Kinloch and Other African American Settlements in St. Ferdinand Township

by Andrew Theising

Missouri Senator John B. Henderson, of Louisiana MO, authored the 13th Amendment of the Constitution (Scharf 1497-98). Many will remember Steven Spielberg's 2012 *Lincoln* biopic, which examined Lincoln's life through the 13th Amendment's battle for passage in the House of Representatives. The Senate version, under Henderson's guidance, had a smoother journey. Its ratification ended slavery in the United States, and along with the 14th and 15th amendments, undid a measure of the "defect" (technically more than functionally) that Thurgood Marshall noted in 1987.

Father Edward Reynolds, S.J., wrote the laudable (yet imperfect) 1949 book *Jesuits for the Negro* to chronicle the history of African American ministry among the Jesuits. It has an interesting chapter on the Jesuits' work in Florissant. One of its strongest contributions is its documentation of the several small communities of African Americans that arose around Florissant. This work, coupled with more recent analyses, allows for brief sketches of these communities.

North County: Always a Significant Population

North St. Louis County has always had a significant African American population, both enslaved and free. According to Scharf's history of St. Louis County, the 1828 Missouri census identified 2,439 people living in St. Ferdinand Township, and 496 of them were either enslaved or free persons of color, the latter making up about 15-20% of that number by the 1840s. In 1860, the colored population of St. Ferdinand Township was 863. By 1870, after emancipation, it was 952. For both of those years, St. Ferdinand Township had the largest colored population of any township in St. Louis County, and in 1860 its colored population was larger than any single ward in the City of St. Louis as well. (Scharf, pp. 1015-1020)

Dr. John A. Wright Sr. has written several fine volumes on the history of Kinloch and other African American communities, and this work is intended to complement, not duplicate, his volumes. He has built a strong foundation of scholarship on which this work rests. Thank you, Dr. Wright, for your work over many decades.

The Old Town Florissant Settlement

There was "a little settlement near St. Ferdinand's in Florissant, where some of the old slaves of the novitiate lived" (Reynolds 94). There is anecdotal evidence that an African American community existed at the north end of Rue St. Charles. Taken together, the likely place for this community would have been on St. Louis University property that was located on the very edge of Old Town—today along Lindbergh Boulevard between St. Charles Street and Jefferson Street, all the way south to St. Ferdinand. There was also a cemetery on this property that was distinct from the historic burial grounds at today's Spanish Land Grant Park. The burial ground would have been on the northern end of Rue St. Ferdinand near the present day entrance drive to St. Ferdinand Park.

There is a question if the burial ground was ever used. Carol Kane of Historic Florissant Inc. suggests that it might have been a temporary location after the time the original cemetery was forced to close (Spanish Land Grant Park) and before the new Saint Ferdinand Cemetery (along Graham Road) was organized and opened. Though lots were sold in the temporary cemetery, it is unclear if there were ever burials there. There is no record of burial or removal, though records of sale are mentioned.

There were enough children living in the area for the pastor of St. Ferdinand's church to establish a Sunday school program for African Americans from 1885 to 1893 at the church. Jesuit novices reported instructing 17 African American children, presumably during this same time period (Reynolds 95).

The Charbonier Road Settlement

As early as 1865, there was a dedicated chapel for African American worship at Florissant being staffed by the Jesuits. It was on the second floor of an existing log/frame building that is further identified in Kelly Schmidt's work (see shmr.jesuits.org, and references in Chapter Three of this book). It is speculated that the large group of enslaved people at St. Stanislaus attracted a community of African Americans in the nearby area. Dr. John Wright associates a log church structure with Sandtown, and reproduced the historic photo in his 2005 book *St. Louis: Disappearing Black Communities*. The historic photo may not be the same building as the Jesuit chapel.

Reynolds notes a small settlement of African Americans in the bottomland near the seminary property as early as 1869 (Reynolds 94). The Seminary property noted by Fr. Reynolds was not the Seminary buildings on Howdershell, but rather the retreat property that is today the conservation area of that name.

This community along the Missouri River may be linked to the **"Sandtown"** settlement described by Dr. John Wright. An 1898 newspaper article locates Sandtown being at the old railroad bridge heading into St. Charles (near present day Highway 370 bridge). St. Ferdinand Church records mention several African Americans living in the **"St. Charles Bottoms,"** presumably the Missouri River bottomland across from St. Charles. So this settlement of African Americans may have spread across a distance of a few miles along the southern bank of the Missouri River, from today's Highway 370 bridge to today's St. Stanislaus Conservation Area. The Charbonier/Aubuchon/Missouri Bottom Road parallels the settlement zone.

There is very little additional information about this settlement.

The Musick's Ferry Settlement

By 1886, the Jesuits were conducting mission work with African Americans at Musick's Ferry approximately where present-day New Halls Ferry ends at the Missouri River. Reynolds described it as being "quite distant" from St. Stanislaus (which it was), and it therefore limited the amount of work that could be done there. (Reynolds 95)

This may be the same area described by Father Callaghan in 1867 as not having "a single Catholic family among them," rather Baptist or Methodist instead. We know from other records that Protestant missionaries were both active and successful in this area (consider, for example, the pioneering work of Rev. John Clark who is buried at the Cold Water Cemetery).

See Cindy Winkler's essay on the slaveholding Patterson and Musick families, whose enslaved people continued to reside in this part of St. Ferdinand Township in Chapter Three of this book. Peggy Kruse's thoughtful history *Old Jamestown Across the Ages* also speaks to this area's history.

The Robertson Settlement (Anglum)

A rather large community of African Americans settled in the Robertson area, then known as Anglum, about three miles south of St. Stanislaus Seminary. The records are scarce, but Reynolds notes that the Jesuits baptized one man there as far back as 1871. By 1919, the faith community there had blossomed into St. Peter Claver chapel. Jesuits would come from the seminary to administer sacraments and provide religious education. By 1922, the small chapel was enlarged to a capacity of 400 people. In the 1930s, the Helpers of Holy Souls sisters came to the community and added vocational and social programs. They had a small but growing population. From a Catholic community of 60 in 1935, there were 120 by 1944 and 140 by 1946. (Reynolds 97-99)

The work expanded in 1944 when a school was built, which served 40 children. The School Sisters of Notre Dame sent five sisters to work there and also at the mission in South Kinloch. (Reynolds 99) The modern development of Lambert St. Louis International Airport, and the surrounding industrial land uses, has meant the destruction of much of these historic African American communities. (See also the African American Greenwood Cemetery in this area, with history dating back to 1874, at www.greenwoodstl.org for additional history.)

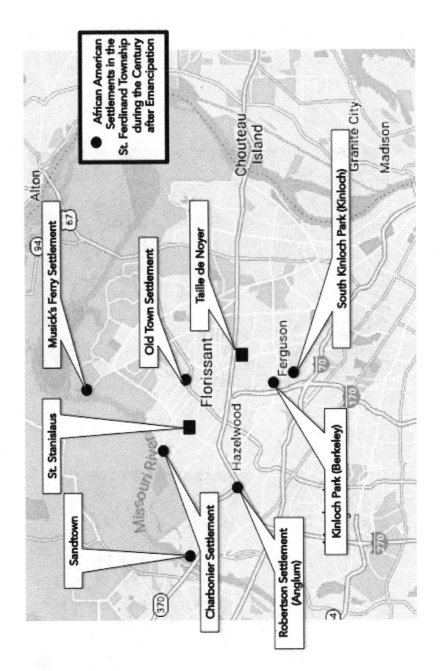

Theising graphic

70

Notes and Sources for this section:

Reynolds, Edward D., S.J. *Jesuits for the Negro*. New York: The America Press, 1949.

Scharf, Thomas. *A History of St. Louis City and County*. Philadelphia: L. H. Everts, 1883.

Wright, John. *St. Louis: Disappearing Black Communities*. Charleston: Arcadia Publishing, 2005.

Above: aerial view of the Holy Angels complex in South Kinloch Park, c. 1940. Below: Children at St. Peter Claver Mission Church in Anglum. From The Church at Work, public domain.

The History of Kinloch

The largest and most permanent settlement was at Kinloch. It was about three miles east of Anglum and eight miles south from St. Stanislaus. Father Reynolds notes that it was a growing community: by 1923 there were 2,300 inhabitants, by 1927 the number grew to 3,600, and the growth continued into the 1940s. (1) The Holy Angels church was established there to serve the growing African American population.

The Origins of the Place Called "Kinloch"

The name "Kinloch" came from James Lucas Turner's horse farm, moved from other locations to what is now the vicinity of Kinloch, MO about 1883. Here he bred prize-winning racehorses, perhaps the finest race horses in the United States. The animals fetched high prices (equivalent to $50,000 today) and gained Turner a national reputation. (2)

Turner was descended from the Lucas and Hunt families. His mother was Julia Mary Hunt (1822-1900). Descendants of her brother Charles Lucas Hunt (1820-1885), who also was a racehorse enthusiast, built the Wilson Price Hunt House on Natural Bridge Road. Turner's father was Captain Henry Smith Turner (1811-1881), a descendant of the Randolphs of Virginia. He married Bertha Gabriella Chouteau (1853-1937), a direct descendant of the founder of St. Louis.

Kinloch Farm was a prosperous piece of land containing at least 334 acres and perhaps as much as 436. The January family in Ferguson had owned it previously, but at the time of Kinloch Farm J. V. Williamson of Philadelphia leased the land to Turner. Turner contracted typhoid and died at age 33 in 1888. His widow purchased the land from Williamson, and then conveyed the land to Sarah Chambers, widow of a Mullanphy descendant and resident of Taille de Noyer since 1881. Chambers paid $100 an acre. All of the horse stock was sold off to others and the farm closed. (3)

Within a year, investors were approaching Mrs. Chambers with offers to create a suburban town on the site. A newspaper feature noted: "A prettier or more convenient site for a suburban village would be difficult to find, and parties recognizing its natural beauties and the railway advantages it has have been trying to buy it from Mrs. Chambers and it is reported that they have about succeeded." (4) A consortium did succeed in buying the undeveloped pastureland and called the place "Kinloch Park."(5) They paid $150 an acre, giving Mrs. Chambers a 50% profit on that part of her investment after only 18 months. The vision for this residential portion was to create a suburban community with lots ranging from two to five acres.

Other Kinloch Development

The remaining land of Kinloch Farm, which could have been from 60 to 125 acres, underwent several changes in land use and ownership. A group stepped forward to purchase the homestead itself. This was within easy walking distance of the present-day bridge where Hanley Road crosses over the Wabash tracks. The investors wanted to establish a "gentlemen's country club" in the old house and call it "Kinloch Villa." (6) Two of the elite names associated with the venture were Cliff Richardson (drug company executive, founder of Chemical Bank in St. Louis, and man for whom the Art Museum Library is named) and Ellis Wainwright (builder who hired Louis Sullivan to design his Wainwright Building in downtown St. Louis). It was at this Kinloch club that a group of businessmen met in 1896 to form a telephone company to compete with Bell Telephone, and the "Kinloch Telephone Company" was born. (7)

Another part of the acreage had been leased to Robert L. Pate of the Kinloch Jockey Club, who established the Kinloch Track—a use hearkening back to its history as a horse farm. The track was launched in 1900 and was later called the Florissant Valley Jockey Club, but was not profitable once Missouri outlawed horse gambling in 1903. Mr. Pate had an option to buy the land for $250 an acre but it was never exercised. (8)

Additional Kinloch land caught the eye of Albert Bond Lambert and the St. Louis Aero Club in 1909, as they scouted for a place to host a planned aviation meet the following year. Newspapers reported that this land was on the site of the old horse track. Technically, according to former County historian David Gonzalez, the airfield and the horse track were on near-adjacent lots. The Frost family owned the land for this, inheritors to Graham's Hazelwood estate. The aero group called their space "Kinloch Field" and they were eager to establish a flying field. Ex-president Theodore Roosevelt became the first president to fly in a plane when he visited Kinloch Field for the international aviation exposition in 1910. The land was renamed Lambert Field and subsequently expanded into today's modern airport a few miles to the west. (9)

African American Settlement at Kinloch

About this same time, some of the lots beyond the south border of Kinloch Park were being sold to African Americans. There was a park on that end of town, Lix Park, which was for the use of these residents. As a publicity stunt, the developers brought in J. Arthur Headon, believed to be the only African American pilot at the time, to give a flight exhibition for prospective buyers. (10) "South Kinloch Park" was a subdivision sold exclusively to African Americans. One article reported 1,500 lots had been sold "to the better class of St. Louis negroes" in 1911, with about 10% of them having built a house already. Another article noted that 1,200 to 1,500 people visited Lix Park each weekend. (11)

There was genuine demand for housing among African Americans. Segregation and deed covenants prevented many from having meaningful choices when it came to home style or location. These new homes offered that choice and homebuyers flocked to the new community. Sadly, some white land speculators sought to make exorbitant profits and took advantage of the new homebuyers. Still, the homes sold steadily and within 20 years, there were about 5,000 African Americans living in South Kinloch Park. (12)

After the 1917 pogrom in East St. Louis—which was the country's bloodiest racial violence ever—many African American families relocated to the new suburb. Like locations in East St. Louis, it was close to transportation and jobs. Race relations were tense in Metro East. Segregation in Illinois was illegal, but it happened anyway. Kinloch, somewhat like nearby Brooklyn IL, offered African Americans a dedicated jurisdiction that even held out the potential for self-governance.

The Struggle for Incorporation

The area known as South Kinloch Park incorporated as the City of Kinloch in 1948 as the first Black city in the state (and how many could there have been nationwide?—it was a great achievement). It was a difficult path, though, and the city almost didn't make it. It all started in February of 1947, when 1,200 residents filed a petition with the County Court, which was then the mechanism for creating a new city. The hearing went well, according to Kinloch attorney T. Douglas Moore, but the court "suddenly changed its attitude." (13) The court denied the petition, claiming the petition was defective. The petition was re-filed in April and three more hearings were held. Finally, on August 20, 1948, the City of Kinloch was established. Willie Head became the city's first mayor.

Mayor Head immediately convened a mass rally at Dunbar Elementary School, to introduce the new elected officials and "thank the Lord for incorporation" he proclaimed. (14) As soon as things started coming together for the new city, it all started to unravel.

An opposition group had argued against incorporation in 1948. In 1949, a new petition was filed—this time with 2,000 signatures—to disincorporate Kinloch on the grounds it was too poor to survive as a city. The County Court agreed, and on June 1, 1949, ordered the new city to be dissolved. Kinloch had lasted only nine months. (15)

The mayor was flummoxed. The city's attorney filed an immediate appeal the decision to the County Court. That October, a judge heard the mayor's appeal and still upheld the disincorporation—no more Kinloch. Soon, a new hearing was requested for December. Again, the judge denied it and upheld the disincorporation. The city then appealed to the Missouri Supreme Court.

All the while, the city continued to operate under the various appeals and the time had come for the city's first election in 1950. There were seven vacancies on the Board of Aldermen. Seven men filed as candidates who were all part of the Citizens Civic League of Kinloch, and all of them favored disincorporation. They would use their new seats to close down the city for good. (16) The scheme was unsuccessful.

The Missouri Supreme Court ruled in July 1951 that the disincorporation petitions were not compliant with state law. The case was remanded, functionally reversing the County's decision and allowing Kinloch to keep its status as a city. Recall that this was the old "South Kinloch Park."

Racial Division between Neighbors

Racial division showed itself a decade before this. Whites had already formalized a split between the old "Kinloch Park" and "South Kinloch Park" when the original Kinloch Park incorporated as the city of Berkeley, MO on July 29, 1937. The Jockey Club track, the Aero Club grounds, and the Kinloch Villa were all in this area incorporated as Berkeley.

The name came from the Berkeley Acres subdivision that had been developed in the area back in 1920 to serve workers in the factories along Natural Bridge Road. (17) Residents then renamed their community "Nuroad" to distinguish the old Kinloch Park from South Kinloch Park. They succeeded in having the Post Office there renamed in 1928 but never incorporated formally.

Schools became an immediate concern. The potential location of a high school for African American students in the northern section of the school district prompted concerns. White residents had attempted to create their own school district separate from South Kinloch's, but were unsuccessful. The County Court did not see sufficient justification to allow a separate school district at the time. This was a primary motivation for pursuing municipal incorporation. The new Berkeley School District was created within a month of the city's incorporation. (18)

Berkeley struggled to keep its incorporation though. Like Kinloch's experience in 1949, petitioners moved to disincorporate Berkeley almost as soon as it was created. The *Globe-Democrat* headline described the situation well: "City of Berkeley: Born of Strife, Up in Arms Again." Once the first tax bills were issued in 1938, residents balked. They felt high tax rates would diminish the city's potential in the future and noted that the new school district (which had been the true goal of many) would remain after the city disincorporated. (19) The move was unsuccessful but it showed how litigious the parties could be.

Samuel W. Fordyce Jr. (1877-1948), an attorney and son of a prominent railroad tycoon, was Berkeley's first mayor. He had married Harriet Frost (1876-1960), daughter of General Daniel Marsh Frost, and they were the last family to reside in the old mansion named Hazelwood that had previously been the Graham plantation. (20)

Side-by-Side

The two cities have existed side-by-side for most of a century, though the population of Berkeley is quite diverse and the remaining schools are all combined. Kinloch peaked in population in the 1960 census, with 6,501 residents. Airport land buyouts in the 1980s decimated the land and population, to the point where less than 300 residents remain today. Berkeley peaked in population in the 1970 census, at just fewer than 20,000 residents. It population has since declined to just under 8,900 but remains larger than Kinloch ever was. In 1975, under court order, the Berkeley and Kinloch School Districts merged with the Ferguson-Florissant School District.

Kinloch's history is recorded well by Dr. John A. Wright Sr., once the superintendent of the Kinloch School District. See, for example, Wright's *Kinloch: Missouri's First Black City* (Arcadia Publishing Black America Series, 2000) and *St. Louis: Disappearing Black Communities* (Arcadia, 2005).

The editor is grateful to Dr. John A. Wright Sr. for his contributions to this work, especially to this essay. He has meticulously documented the African American history of St. Louis and those of us who follow him owe a debt of gratitude. Dr. Wright's lifelong dedication to education and knowledge is a model for us all.

Notes for the Kinloch History:

1. Reynolds 99-100

2. "Sporting Notes," St Louis Globe-Democrat, 11 Apr 1886, p. 10; and "Horse Chat," St. Louis Post-Dispatch 11 Jan 1884, p. 5. *There has been speculation that the African American settlement at Kinloch, which became Missouri's first African American city, was somehow associated with Richard Graham's estate and perhaps his Scottish heritage. While the name can be found on the East Coast where his family was from, there is nothing in the historical record to indicate a link between Graham and Kinloch. Additionally, there was a competitive racehorse of the 1880 era called "Kinlock" or "Kinloch," but it is unclear if that horse was tied to this horse farm.*

3. see "The Sale of Kinloch Confirmed," *St. Louis Post-Dispatch*, 11 Jan 1889, p. 3. Another article references a sale price of $125 an acre, but the article informed by Mrs. Turner said $100. Chambers residing at Taille comes from: Society News, *St. Louis Globe-Democrat*, 10 Apr 1881, p. 10.

4. "A New Town Site of 300 Acres," St. Louis Post-Dispatch, 13 Apr 1889, pg. 5.

5. "Kinloch Park Purchasers and Their Prospective Improvements," *St. Louis Post-Dispatch*, 02 Jul 1890, p. 2.

6. "Kinloch Villa Purchased...," *St. Louis Post-Dispatch* 28 Apr 1892 p. 11.

7. See "Kinloch History Part 1," at https://southsidespaces. com/kinloch-history-part-1/

8. "Kinloch Park Title Suit," *St. Louis Globe-Democrat*, 02 Sep 1910, p. 13; and Gonzalez, David. "At Kinloch Field...," *St. Louis Magazine.* 02 Jan 2018.

9. Gonzalez, David. "At Kinloch Field...," *St. Louis Magazine.* 02 Jan 2018.

10. "Negro to Make Flights," *St. Louis Post-Dispatch* 30 Oct 1912 p. 6.

11. "Negro to Make Flights," *St. Louis Post-Dispatch* 30 Oct 1912, p. 6; and "Negroes in County Object...," *St. Louis Post-Dispatch* 22 Jun 1919 p. 31.

12. "Lots White Men Buy Doubled in Price to Negroes," St. Louis Post-Dispatch 24 Jan 1917, p. 3.

13. "County Court Denies Kinloch Park...," St. Louis Star Times 11 Jul 1947 p. 24.

14. Missouri's Only All-Negro City..." *St. Louis Globe-Democrat* 26 Aug 1948 pg. 3.

15. "City of Kinloch in County Disincorporated...," *St. Louis Post-Dispatch* 01 Jun 1949, p. 18.

16. "Seven to File at Kinloch...," *St. Louis Star Times* 03 Mar 1950, p. 15.

17. See in Web Archive "St. Louis County Place Names," State Historical Society of Missouri, https://web.archive.org/web/20160624071311/http://shsmo.org/manuscripts/ramsay/ramsay_saint_louis.html and "New Subdivision...," *St. Louis Post-Dispatch* 04 Apr 1920, p. 9.

18. "Berkeley Now City in County," *St. Louis Globe-Democrat* 30 Jul 1937, p. 2.

19. "Move to Dissolve...," *St. Louis Post-Dispatch.* 25 Oct 1938, p. 11.

20. See "Samuel Wesley Fordyce," *Findagrave* (https://www. findagrave.com/memorial/49485687/samuel-wesley-fordyce)

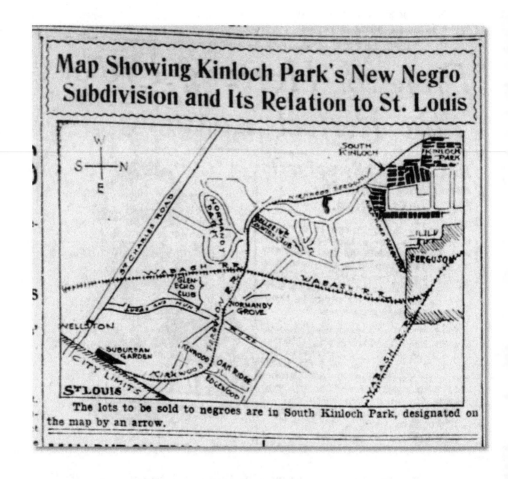

Map Showing Kinloch Park's New Negro Subdivision and Its Relation to St. Louis

The lots to be sold to negroes are in South Kinloch Park, designated on the map by an arrow.

Above: Feature on South Kinloch from 1917, the year many African Americans fled East St. Louis's racial violence and moved to St. Louis County. Newspapers.com

1892 advertisement for some of the earliest residential land sales at Kinloch Park. Newspapers.com

COURT DENIES A PETITION TO INCORPORATE KINLOCH

A petition to incorporate Kinloch, Negro community, as a fourth class city was denied by the St. Louis County Court today on the ground that the petition was improperly drawn.

Sat., Aug. 21, 1948

Kinloch Becomes Missouri's First All-Negro City

Kinloch, a community in northwest St. Louis County between Berkley and Ferguson, became the first all-Negro city in Missouri yesterday when its incorpo-

said.

CITY OF KINLOCH IN COUNTY DISINCORPORATED BY COURT

The fourth-class city of Kinloch, only incorporated Negro community in St. Louis county, was disincorporated today by the County Court. Notice of appeal to the Circuit Court was filed by

Disincorporation of Kinloch Reversed

By a Globe-Democrat Staff Writer
JEFFERSON CITY, MO., July 9.—The Missouri Supreme Court today reversed a St. Louis County Circuit Court order disincorporating the City of Kinloch in the northern part of the county and ordered the matter retried.
Evidence presented before the County Court and later on appeal

Four headlines show the on-again, off-again struggle to incorporate Kinloch.
Newspapers.com

African American or Mulatto Residents in the 1870 Census for Certain Portions of St. Ferdinand Township

(noting those living in or next to white households known to have been slaveholding families)

Compiled by Cindy Winkler

The tables beginning on the next page have rows that are shaded by census household entry (and the "notes" box crosses all rows associated with a single household). Only nonwhite household members are listed.

The census page number can be seen on the associated file housed on the FVHS web page. The proximity on the census page does not guarantee that a relationship existed; it is only speculation. This may not be a complete listing.

The entries were kept in page order, rather than in alphabetical order, to preserve the sequence of people's locations. The census generally was done one household after another along the same road or tract. Hence, two families listed on the same page likely lived on adjacent or nearby properties.

Some of the handwriting is difficult to decipher. When searching for ancestors or specific individuals, it works best to pursue variations in spellings. Scans of the original handwritten documents that informed this table are to be posted on the FVHS web page under "galleries." The complete census is available online through various providers, like Ancestry.com.

Name of African American Citizen (M)=Mulatto	Age	Gender	Birth	Occupation	White Neighbor (N) or Household (H) Name	Census Page	Notes
Morse, Henry	30	M	MO		Price, Frederic (H)	13	
Washington, George	38	M	KY	Laborer	Hanley, Samuel (N)	27	
Washington, Flora	22	F	MO	Housekeeper		27	
Washington, George	2	M	MO			27	
Washington, Jennie	10/12	F	MO			27	
Addison, Grace	20	M	MO		Redman, James (H)	28	
Hyatt, Harris	40	M	MO	Laborer	Hyatt, Pemilise (N)	28	
Hyatt, Julia (M)	40	F	MO	Housekeeper		28	Child Louis was not designated (M) like the other children, suggesting separate parentage.
Hyatt, Perry (M)	11	M	MO			28	
Hyatt, Florence (M)	8	F	MO			28	
Hyatt, Louis	6	M	MO			28	
Hyatt, Nanny (M)	2	F	MO			28	
Taylor, Walter (M)	5	M	MO			30	(incomplete entry; begins on page 29) only Walter is (M)
Taylor, Laura	3	F	MO			30	

Name	Age	Sex	BP	Occupation	Household	Age	Notes
Crowelle?, John	30	M	MO	Laborer	Crowelle?, John (H)	30	
Harris, Mary Jane	20	F	MO	Servant	Gossiah?, Charles (H)	30	
Ventzen, William	30	M	MO	Laborer		30	
Ventzen, Lucy	25	F	MO	Housekeeper		30	
Ventzen, Julia	10	F	MO			30	
Ventzen, Clara	5	F	MO			30	
Clements, Lee	10	M	MO		Walker, James (H)	30	
Douglas, Jane	24	F	MO	Servant	Douglas, Nicholas (H)	45	
Daretwood?, Jenny	74	F	MO		Blackburn, Rufus (H)	45	
Nelson, Frank	27	M	MO	Laborer	Valle, Jacob (H) Page 47	48	
Austin, George	47	M	MO	Laborer		48	
Brown, Alice	12	F	MO	Nurse	Owens, John (H)	49	
Tunstall, Washington	65	M	VA	Laborer			Elizabeth Musick, age 82, white, is listed as part of Tunstall's household
Harrison, Easter	25	F	MO	Laborer		49	
Harrison, Susan	12	F	MO			50	
Harrison, Amanda	5	F	MO			50	

Name	Age	Sex	State	Occupation	Household	No.	Notes
Binsen, Henry (M)	27	M	MO	Laborer	Hume, George (N)	50	Hume family above and below their entry
Binsen, Delia (M)	22	F	MO	Housekeeper		50	
Wilburn, Thomas	29	M	MO	Laborer	St. Cyr, Pascal (N)	86	Mr. Wilburn had a white Frenchman living in his household, Peter Roradan, 25.
Wilburn, Katharine	23	F	MO	Housekeeper		86	
Wilburn, George	15	M	MO			86	
Wilburn, Charles	12	M	MO			86	
Wilburn, Jennie	10	F	MO			86	
Jefferson, Thomas	40	M	VA	Laborer		86	
Jefferson, Edward	20	M	VA	Laborer		86	
[Li]noball, Isaac	25	M	VA	Laborer		86	
Magen, Harriet	40	F	KY	Servant		86	
Carson, Matilda	26	F	VA	Servant	Gibson, James (H)	87	
Carson, Dudley	6	M	MO			87	
Carson, Eddie	5	M	MO			87	
Carson, Divina	3	F	MO			87	
Foster, William	28	M	MO	Laborer		87	
Turner, Jake	36	M	KY	Laborer		87	
Turner, Jane	27	F	KY	Servant		87	
Turner, Amanda	8	F	MO			87	
Turner, William	6	M	MO			87	
Turner, Henry	4	M	MO			87	

Name	Age	Sex	Birthplace	Occupation		Page	Notes
Foster, William	30	M	MO	Laborer		87	
Foster, Alice	26	F	MO	Housekeeper		87	
Foster, Harriet	7	F	MO			87	
Foster, Julius	4	M	MO			87	
Foster, Emma	3	F	MO			87	
Foster, Laura	1	F	MO			87	
Mayhew, Sarah	24	F	MO	At home		87	
Mossby, Jake	50	M	VA	Farmer		87	
Mossby, Milla	21	F	MO	Housekeeper		87	
Mossby, Katharine	1	F	MO			87	
Jonas, Ellen	22	F	AR			87	
Vanderburgh, D.	40	M	AR	Farmer		87	
Vanderburgh, Ellen	30	F	AR	Housekeeper		87	
McNeil, Isaac	58	M	MO	Laborer		87	Mr. McNeil had a white child, Hiram Greenway, age 5, living in household
McNeil, Amanda	50	F	MO	Housekeeper		87	
McNeil, Annalia	16	F	MO	At home		87	
McNeil, Henry	9	M	MO			87	
Williams, John	30	M	MO	Laborer	Bissell, James (H)	92	
Taylor, Sarah	48	F	MO	Servant		92	
Alice, Francis	40	M	MO	Servant		92	
Alice, Wierine	72	F	MO	Servant		92	
Alice, Eddie	11	M	MO	Servant		92	

86

Name	Age	Sex	Birthplace	Occupation	Household	No.	Notes
Francis, Michael	23	M	MO	Laborer	Harris, James (H); Musick Reuben (N)	95	For more on the Francis family, see the Winkler essay in Chapter 3.
Balte, Joseph	12	M	MO	Laborer		95	
White, Nick	34	M	MO	Laborer	Musick Reuben (N)	95	
White, Jane	28	F	MO	Housekeeper		95	
White, Charles	4	M	MO			95	
Wheeler, Francis	24	M	KY	Laborer	Musick Reuben (N)	95	Elizabeth Musick, age 82, is listed as part of this household; she is also listed in the Tunstall household.
Wheeler, Martha	26	F	MO	Housekeeper		95	
Wheeler, Samuel (M)	3	M	MO			95	
Trammel, Clara	70	F	VA	Servant	Hyatt, James (H)	100	
Trammel, Henson	45	M	VA	Laborer		100	
Woodruff, Isaac	60	M	VA	Farmer		100	
Woodruff, Harriet	55	F	MO	Housekeeper		100	
Black, Edward	28	M	MO	Farmer		124	
Black, Amanda	26	F	MO	Housekeeper		124	
Black, Nancy	14	F	MO	Housekeeper		124	
Black, Dennis	11	M	MO	Housekeeper		124	
Black, Caroline	5	F	MO			124	

Name	Age	Sex	Birthplace	Occupation		
Black, Julia	4	F	MO		124	(continued from previous table)
Black, Emanuel	1	F	MO		124	
Young, Mary	50	F	MO		124	
Porter, Reuben	67	M	VA	Farmer	124	
Porter, Sophia	50	F	KY	Housekeeper	124	
Porter, Henry W.	26	M	MO		124	
Porter, Minnie	12	F	MO		124	
Stone, Charles	35	M	MO	Farmer	124	
Stone, Martha	30	F	MO	Housekeeper	124	
Stone, Mary	12	F	MO		124	
Stone, Griffin	8	M	MO		124	
Stone, Denene	7	F	MO		124	
Goodwin, Albert	35	M	MO	Farmer	124	
Goodwin, Margaret	30	F	MO	Housekeeper	124	
Goodwin, Albert W.	5/12	M	MO		124	
William, Hiram	11	M	MO			
Reed, Henry	62	M	VA	Laborer	124	
Reed, Juddie	63	F	VA	Housekeeper	124	
Reed, Henry	18	M	MO	Laborer	124	
Reed, Missouri	16	F	MO	At home	124	
Black, Dennis	24	M	MO	Laborer	124	
Black, Lizzy	4	F	MO		124	

Name	Age	Sex	State	Occupation	Other	Page	Notes
Black, Cossby	50	M	MO	Farmer		124	
Black, Eliza	18	F	MO	Housekeeper		124	
Black, Mary	16	F	MO	Housekeeper		124	Four members of the household from four states
White, John	48	M	PA	Laborer		135	
White, Barbara	52	F	MD	Housekeeper		135	
White, Martha	16	F	AL			135	
White, Ida	1	F	MO			135	
Lent, Alfred	35	M	MO	Laborer		135	
Lent, Lavina	40	F	MO	Housekeeper		135	
Lent, Fannie	8	F	MO			135	
Pruett, Marietta	38	M	MO	Laborer		135	
Bentley, Pollie	83	F	VA	Servant	Thomas, Daniel (H)	135	
Bentley, Charles	11	M	MO			135	
Red, Charles	30	M	KY	Laborer		136	
Red, Martha	30	F	KY	Housekeeper		136	
Red, Kate	10	F	MO			136	
Red, Florence	2	F	MO			136	
Patterson, Robert	23	M	MO	Laborer		136	St. Stanislaus Seminary
Queen, Joseph	40	M	MO	Laborer		138	
Queen, Peter	35	M	MO	Laborer		138	
Queen, Charlotte	32	F	MO	Laborer		138	St. Stanislaus Seminary
Queen, Mary	58	F	MD	Laborer		138	
Harmon?, Richard	60	M	MO	Laborer		138	
Harmon, Samuel	40	M	MD	Laborer		138	

Name	Age	Sex	Birthplace	Occupation	Household	Page	Notes
Harmon, Thomas	16	M	MO	Laborer		138	(continued from previous table)
Harmon, Richard	7	M	MO	Laborer		138	
Harmon, Adelain	4	M	MO	Laborer		138	
Harmon, Edmond	2	M	MO	Laborer		138	
Jackson, Clay	40	M	VA	Laborer		138	
Jackson, Susan	35	F	KY	Housekeeper		138	This would be in the vicinity of St. Stanislaus.
Jackson, Thomas	18	M	MO	Laborer		138	
Jackson, Abraham	16	M	MO	Laborer		138	
Jackson, Wilhelmina	12	F	MO			138	
Jackson, Elizabeth	8	F	MO			138	
Powell, Margaret	20	F	MO	Servant	Rose, Louis (H)	164	
Ware, Frederick	40	M	MO	Laborer	Jackson, Mallet (H)	164	
White, Martha	16	F	MO	Servant	Wash, E. L. (H)	164	
Ferguson, Isaac	30	M	AL		Ferguson, William (H)	164	
Gray, Rosetta	60	F	KY	Servant	Chambers, Jane (H)	166	This is the Taille de Noyer household. One servant from Mexico.
Shea, Denny	16	M	MO	Servant		166	
Wilson, John	6	M	MO	Servant		166	
Benton, Thomas	48	M	KY	Servant		166	
Boas, Frank (M)	19	M	Mex	Servant		166	

Name	Age	Sex	Birthplace	Occupation	Household	Page	Notes
Hall, Humphrey	30	M	TN	Laborer		166	
Hall, Frances	25	F	TN	Housekeeper	Chambers, Jane (N)	166	This would be in the vicinity of Taille de Noyer.
Hall, Abraham	10	M	MO			166	
Hall, Mary	9	F	MO			166	
Limms, Thomas	35	M	MD	Servant	Farrar, Anne (H)	166	
Brown, Roberta	35	F	MO	Servant	Moore, Levi (H)	167	
Lane, Luke	23	M	MO	Laborer	Hyatt, Joseph (H)	167	
Willard, Thomas	30	M	MO	Laborer	Gardner, Thomas (N)	167	
Willard, Katharine	28	F	MO	Servant		167	
Willard, George	13	M	MO			167	
Willard, Charles	10	M	MO			167	
Willard, Jennie	7	F	MO			167	
Willard, Mary	14	F	MO	Servant		167	
Traneball?, Mather	45	M	MO	Laborer		167	
Williams, Anderson	43	M	VA	Laborer	Gardner, Thomas (N)	168	
Williams, Lakes	38	F	VA	Housekeeper		168	
Williams, Ellen	17	F	MO	At home		168	
Williams, Frances	15	F	MO	At home		168	
Williams, Emma	13	F	MO			168	
Williams, Matilda	10	F	MO			168	

Name	Age	Sex	Birthplace	Occupation	Household	Page	Notes
Williams, Thomas	8	M	MO			168	(continued from previous table)
Williams, Maggie	4	F	MO			168	
Williams, Arthur	3	F	MO			168	
Williams, Ida	7/12	F	MO			168	
Brown, Aaron	21	M	AR	Laborer		176	Incomplete record (begins on 175)
Scott, Wash	25	M	MO	Laborer		176	
Taylor, Cecelia	16	F	KY	Servant		176	
Graham, Sallie	30	F	MO	Cook	Graham, L. E. (H)	176	
Grant, Stephen	40	M	MO	Laborer	Graham, L. E. (N)	176	
Grant, Lizzie	36	F	MO	Housekeeper		176	
Grant, Lizzie	6	F	MO			176	
Grant, Elize	4	F	MO			176	
Grant, Susan	2	F	MO			176	
Hinds, Pressy	25	F	MO	Servant	Utz, Franklin (N)	180	Incomplete record (begins on 179)
Hinds, Nelle	24	F	MO			180	
Owens, Timothy (M)	55	M	VA	Laborer		180	
Owens, Alfred	40	M	VA	Laborer		180	
Owens, Hannah	7	F	VA			180	
Edmonde, Charles	25	M	MO	Laborer	Utz, Franklin (H)	180	
Edmonde, Harry	26	M	MO	Laborer		180	
Edmonde, Birdy	25	F	MO	Cook		180	

Cheek, Nellie	14	F	MO	Nurse	181
Cheek, Emma	12	F	MO	Nurse	181
Cheek, Margaret	25	F	MO	Nurse	181
Johnson, Jesse	30	M	MO	Laborer	181
Scott, Harrison	40	M	MO	Laborer	181

Rayburn, Frank (H)

Burials of African Americans from St. Ferdinand's Church and Saint Ferdinand Cemetery Records

Compiled by Carol Kane, Historic Florissant Inc.

Carol Kane compiled this record from her review of church and cemetery records starting decades ago. It is difficult work and the records are not always legible, so this list is most but likely not all of the entries. Father Judocus Van Assche, S.J., longtime pastor of St. Ferdinand's, performed most of the burials. The page numbers refer to the actual register page, which is organized by date.

Mrs. Kane began this research before many of the modern search tools were available. All of these records are now online as part of the Drouin Collection of French Church Records that is now part of the Ancestry.com website.

Church Records

Page	Date	Entry	Priest
12	26 Oct 1825	Was buried in the burying grounds of this church, **Sam**, a Black man of Mrs. St. Vrain, old about 23 years	Quickenborne
21	31 Mar 1831	Was buried in the church yard at this parish, **Sophia**, about 16 years of age, a Black girl belonging to Mr. John Mullanphy	Van Assche
22	17 Oct 1831	Was buried in the graveyard at this parish, **John**, a colored boy belonging to Mr. Louis Yosty, between 10 or 11 years of age.	Theux

25	___ Sept 1833	Was buried a Black child belonging to Mrs. _____.	Van Assche
25	09 Jan 1834	I buried _____, a Black man belonging to Mr. Pascal Cerre.	Van Assche
26	05 May 1834	Was buried a Black boy belonging to Mr. Thomas Withington (Senior)	Van Assche
26	05 Jul 1834	Was buried the Black boy [belonging] to Mr. Francois Crilis, about 8 years old	Van Assche
26	09 Jul 1834	Was buried a Black boy belonging to Mr. Francois Crilis, about 14 years	Van Assche
27	31 Oct 1834	Was buried **William**, a child to **Isaac** and **Suzanna**, both servants of St. Stanislaus	Van Assche
27	29 Dec 1834	Was buried **Baptiste**, Black servant to Mr. Sanquinnet	Van Assche
27	01 Jan 1835	Was buried the Black servant maid to Mr. Chambers	Van Assche
27	__ Feb 1835	Was buried a small Black child of Mr. Chambers	Van Assche
28	02 Mar 1838	Was buried **Agnes**, a Black service maid to Mr. Baptiste Crilis	Van Assche
28	30 May 1835	Was buried a little child belonging to Mr. Chambers	Busschotts
30	04 Jun 1836	I buried a Black child of the age of thirteen months belonging to Mr. Braseau	Busschotts

32	23 Feb 1837	I buried **Martha**, a Black girl of 30 years, belonging to Mr. Chambers	Van Assche
{32	15 Oct 1837	I buried a child of **Tilde** and **[Frank?]**, colored people	Van Assche}
33	14 Apr 1839	Was buried **Elizabeth Agnes**, 6 years old, a daughter to **Lewis** and **Sara**, the latter a servant of Mr. Chambers	Gelizel
33	02 May 1839	Was buried a Black girl, two years old, daughter of **Louis** and **Sara**, the latter a servant of Mrs. Chambers	Gelizel
37	20 Mar 1841	**Amos Queen**, Black servant of St. Stanislaus	Van Assche
37	27 Jan 1842	A grown Black boy of Francois St. Cin	Van Assche
37	__ Jun 1842	A Black child of Mrs. Harris, a few days old	Van Assche
40	15 Sep 1844	I buried a Black boy of Mr. August Brazeau	Van Assche
43	03 Aug 1846	I buried a Black child of Mr. Bush	Van Assche
45	22 Jan 1848	I buried a Black girl, about 9 years old, servant to ____	Van Assche
46	25 Apr 1849	I buried **Mary**, a Black servant to Mr. Delaurier Fremont	Van Assche
46	21 Jul 1849	I buried **[Bapt.]**, a Black servant to Mr. Harris, about 60 years old	Van Assche
46	[01] Aug 1849	I buried a Black [boy] of Mrs. Bush, 2 years old	Van Assche

47	05 Jan 1850	I buried a Black woman servant of Mr. Montagne	Van Assche
47	30 Apr 1850	I buried a Black child of [**Richard** and ___], servants of St. Stanislaus	Van Assche
48	17 Sep 1850	I buried ___, wife to [**Isaac**], both servants of Mr. Harris	Van Assche
49	[01] Dec 1850	I buried a Black girl of 3 years [old], daughter to **Hiram**, servant for [Mr. M___], and ___, servant of Mr. Chambers	Van Assche
52	18 Dec 1852	I buried **Mary**, wife to **Tom**, servants of St. Stanislaus	Van Assche
{52	16 Jan 1853	I buried Mr. Robert Wells, 37 years old, and servant of Mr. John Hartnett, amongst killed in coming from St. Louis	Van Assche} *assuming this is an entry for two people, Wells and a servant*
52	[25] Jan 1853	I buried a Black servant of Mr. Sincenne [St. Cin?], called **Mary**	Van Assche
52	18 Feb 1853	I buried a Black child, 6 months old, a servant of Mr. Charles Chambers	Van Assche
53	31 Aug 1853	I buried **Laura**, a Black child of **young Isaac**, servant of St. Stanislaus, and [unnamed mother] a servant of Mr. [Harney?], about 3 months old	Van Assche
	Note from Mrs. Kane: from this point to September 1857, burials were by Father Florian Sautois, S.J. [there is only one African American burial by him, and it was a person from St. Stanislaus—perhaps ministry to this community changed during Father Van Assche's absence with the one exception that follows.]		

72	14 May 1857	I buried **Sally**, Black woman from the novitiate house, age about 60 years	Sautois
76	09 Jan 1859	I buried the mortal remains of a Black girl, servant of Francois St. Cin	Van Assche
80	02 Nov 1862	I buried a Black child of Mr. Alvarez	Van Assche
81	15 Jan 1862	I buried **Eliza**, Black servant of Loretto Academy, about 25 years old	Van Assche
81	20 Feb 1862	I buried **Alfred**, Black servant of Mr. Bogart	Van Assche
82	[no date] June 1853	I buried a Black child of about 1 year, servant of Mrs. Bush	Van Assche
83	25 Apr 1864	I buried **Isaac Queen**, servant of St. Stanislaus, 66 years old	Van Assche
89	18 Apr 1869	I buried **Crotus**, a Black servant who died at St. Stanislaus, over 100 years old	Van Assche
{92	13 Apr 1873	I buried **Margaritte Copes** (a colored girl) 31 years	Van Assche}
{92	16 Apr 1873	I buried ___ called __ , son of **Isaac** and ___	Van Assche}
92	08 May 1873	I buried a Black girl belonging [to the Sisters of the Black ___]	Van Assche
{93	24 Nov 1873	I buried **Jordan Berry**, a colored man who converted himself in his [sickness], husband of a servant formerly belonging to M. [Bush?]	Van Assche}

{94	19 Oct 1874	I buried **Margaritte Woodruff** (colored) about [20(?)] years old	Van Assche}
{94	04 Aug 1875	I buried a Black child a year and ½ old	Van Assche}
{94	13 Dec 1875	I buried a child, one year ___, of a Black man who lives in St. [Charles(?)] Bottom	Van Assche}
{95	23 Jun 1876	I buried a child of a [(crossed-out)] woman, formerly belonging to Mr. William ___	Van Assche}
	[This last child's record almost is the last entry in the book; there were only three other burials entered by Father Van Assche over the next few weeks. He was ailing and would pass away within a year.]		

Cemetery Records

Saint Ferdinand Cemetery (the "new" cemetery on Graham Road established in 1875) had a section reserved for African Americans. It is the southwest section. There is an altar/shrine at the center of the cemetery. Facing the altar/shrine, the north sections are to your right, the south sections to your left; the east sections are behind you and the west sections in front of you.

The African American section of the cemetery, then, is behind the altar and to the left, comprising the first four rows (mostly unmarked). Present-day maps show 13 lots per row, but in the early days of the cemetery there were only about half that number—so the oldest graves are closest to the altar/ shrine.

The first row, notes Mrs. Kane, were the "common" graves for African Americans. (Facing on the opposite side of the street was the row of "common" graves for whites.) These were for indigent persons and are unmarked.

The records for this row indicate the following burials:
- Child, buried 17 Feb 1879
- **Harris, George**, buried 03 Jun 1879
- **Phoenix, Grace**, buried 17 Oct 1879
- **Phoenix, Richard**, buried 11 Apr 1880
- **Phoenix, Edward**, buried 10 Jan 1881
- **Clay, Mary**, buried 20 Mar 1881
- **Berry, Jessie**, buried 28 June 1882
- **Lewis** child, buried 22 Jan 1886
- **Savage**, Mr., buried 25 Dec 1886
- **Lewis** child, buried Aug 1887
- **Phoenix, Jennie**, buried 14 Aug 1887
- **Makin, Mary**, buried 17 Feb 1888
- "Aunt **Rachel**," buried 03 May 1888
- **Phoenix, Henry**, buried 12 Jun 1889
- **Lewis** child, buried August 1890
- **Lewis** child, buried July 1891
- **Clay** child, buried 28 May 1893
- **Maguire** infant, buried 11 Aug 1897

- **Taylor, Ida**, buried 24 Dec 1900
- **Williams, Josephine**, buried 07 Sep 1901
- **Lane, George**, buried 22 Sep 1901
- **Duke, Rose** died 08 Mar 1906 (formerly servant of Mrs. Chambers)
- **O'Brien, James**, died 06 Apr 1936 (formerly servant at St. Stanislaus)

The second and third rows, which have some markings, were divided into lots sold to families. A single lot contained twelve graves, and families could purchase various subdivisions of the lots.

The owner of Row 3 Lot 1 was **Norman and Charlotte Queen** (a surname associated with the first enslaved persons at St. Stanislaus Seminary). Buried here are **Mrs. Mary Queen** (died 12 Feb 1897), **Joseph Queen** (buried 23 Aug 1884), and **Charlotte Queen** (buried July 1891).

Another owner in Row 3 was **Allen Harris** (Lot 2, northeast quadrant containing three graves). Buried here are **Allen Harris** (died 10 Jan 1901, buried 12 Jan 1901), **Eliza Harris** (buried 15 Nov 1889, aged 60 years), and **Arthur Harris** (buried 30 July 1919, aged 43 years, 3 months, 24 days).

Key Court Cases Associated with the Florissant Area

There are three significant civil rights/civil liberties court cases that have their roots in the Florissant Valley. The fact that these cases are rooted in our own back yards illustrates that the Florissant area faces the same issues and attitudes that other areas do across the United States, and that what happens here is indeed of national significance. (The fourth case shows how the landmark *Brown vs. Board of Education* decision was applied to this area.)

These brief summaries are intended to recognize the problems that were raised. All are complex cases and issues—these sketches are intended to provide a direction for individual research and discovery.

Paddock Woods Home Sales Suit
Jones vs. Alfred H. Mayer Co. (1968)

Joseph Lee Jones, an African American man from St. Louis, and his wife, Barbara Jo Jones, a Caucasian woman from Kirkwood, wanted to purchase a home in the Paddock Woods subdivision near I-270 and Highway 367. The sales agent refused to sell them a home solely because of Mr. Jones's race. They filed suit in 1965. Lower courts ruled that home sales were private transactions and sellers could discriminate based on race. The Joneses appealed to the U. S. Supreme Court. Martin Luther King Jr. was assassinated shortly after the hearing began. Congress passed new fair housing rules and on June 17, 1968, the court issued a landmark ruling that declared there is no right to refuse a home sale based on race.

Sadly, the Jones family never was able to purchase a home there. During the years of trial, all of the homes in the subdivision were sold so the family moved to Valencia Drive in Florissant. The couple divorced after 10 years and, tragically in 1974, Mr. Jones was killed in his home by a relative with a mental illness.

Case Source: Tim O'Neil "A St. Louis Couple Wins a Landmark Housing …." *St. Louis Post-Dispatch.* Jun 17 2020. (https://www.stltoday.com/news/local/history/june-17-1968-a-st-louis-couple-wins-a-landmark-housing-rights-case-but-they/article_08928410-2a54-5da6-b749-243ac259a83f.html)

Black Jack Zoning Suit
United States vs. City of Black Jack (1974)

In 1969, the Inter-Religious Center for Urban Affairs (ICUA) moved to purchase 12 acres of land on Old Jamestown Road in unincorporated St. Louis County to create an affordable housing project called Park View Heights. The national government agreed to help fund the project as part of public housing initiatives. Neighbors immediately balked. Fearing an influx of African American residents, organizers launched a municipal incorporation effort to derail the project. The City of Black Jack was formed and passed a zoning ordinance that excluded development like Park View Heights.

Richard Baron, now a well-known developer, was the ACLU attorney who filed suit against Black Jack. The Nixon Administration, under the direction of HUD Secretary George Romney, also filed suit.

The problem, according to the courts, was that race was invoked in the hearings as being a motivator for the action. Even though the zoning law did not explicitly mention racial discrimination, the law had *a discriminatory effect*. Therefore, it was a violation of the 1968 Fair Housing Act and was struck down. Parkview Heights was constructed and the City of Black Jack had to pay the ICUA nearly $500,000.

Case Source: Freivogel, William. "Supreme Court housing discrimination decision had its roots in Black Jack," *St. Louis Public Radio*. (https://news.stlpublicradio. org/government-politics-issues/2015-06-25/supreme-court-housing-discrimination-decision-had-its-roots-in-black-jack)

Hazelwood School Newspaper Suit
Hazelwood School District vs. Kuhlmeier (1988)

While not a social justice case, this was a major Supreme Court decision that started in the Florissant area. Students at Hazelwood East High School wrote a two-page feature for the school newspaper, the *Spectrum*, about how teen pregnancy, runaways, and parental divorce affected students. Cathy Kuhlmeier was the student editor of the paper. Principal Robert Reynolds reviewed the issue before publication, as he always did, and deleted those two pages without informing students of his decision. Students and parents objected to the censorship and filed suit with support of the ACLU. Reynolds claimed it was an inappropriate topic for the newspaper and the feature lacked fairness and balance.

Existing legal interpretation held that students and teachers "did not shed their constitutional rights" when entering a school. However, the Supreme Court ruled that a school newspaper produced as part of a class was not a public forum and that schools could censor student speech for "legitimate pedagogical concern."

The ruling remains a major free-speech decision to this day that is still mentioned in legal cases.

Case Source: McGowan, Bailey. "25 years later, a look at one generation under Hazelwood," *Student Press Law Center*. Posted 14 Jan 2013. (https://splc.org/ 2013/01/25-years-later-a-look-at-one-generation-under-hazelwood/)

The School Desegregation Order

United States vs. State of Missouri, School Districts of Berkeley, Kinloch, Ferguson et al (1975)

Decision of the Eighth Circuit Court of Appeals

By the 1970s, nearly a generation after *Brown vs. Board* (1954), segregation was still a major problem in St. Louis County schools. This was a separate settlement from the case led by Minnie Liddell in 1972 under Judge James H. Meredith, and later settled by Judge William L. Hungate. This is a very complicated and drawn-out case, and deserves more discussion than can be had here. See Gerald Heaney and Susan Uchitelle's *Unending Struggle: The Long Road to an Equal Education in St. Louis* (Reedy Press, 2004). Under the *Liddell* settlements, the City of St. Louis entered into a busing arrangement with school districts in St. Louis County. However, North St. Louis County communities went a different route.

Judge Meredith, the same judge as in the *Liddell* case, responded to a complaint of inferior schools at Kinloch resulting from the deliberate creation and maintenance of "the Kinloch district as an all-Black school district, denying equal opportunity to its students and thereby denying them equal protection of the law." (Justia)

A key finding was that the neighboring districts all had a hand in doing so. Meredith asked for proposals to settle the matter, and the responses suggested a merger of school districts. This, too, is a long and complicated case that deserves more attention that can be given in this summary. Meredith so ordered a merger of school districts on June 7, 1975. Ferguson and Florissant were already combined, and now Berkeley and Kinloch would join them. The adjacent school districts were operating racially segregated schools in violation of the 14th Amendment. (See the story of Kinloch's settlement in Chapter Two for more details on the establishment of these districts.) When the State and the Districts appealed the order, the Eighth Circuit Court of Appeals supported Meredith's order and the merger was completed.

Case Sources: U.S. vs. State of Missouri et al, *Justia.* (https://law.justia.com/cases/federal/appellate-courts/F2/515/1365/292920/); Davis, Chad and Ryan Delaney, "Berkeley Residents Ask…" 07 Dec 2018 (https://news.stlpublicradio.org/show/st-louis-on-the-air/2018-12-07/berkeley-residents-ask-when-you-take-the-schools-away-whats-left); O'Neil, Tim, "Lawsuit Led to Major…," *St. Louis Post-Dispatch* 18 Feb 2020 (https:// www.stltoday.com/news/archives/a-look-back-lawsuit-led-to-major-changes-in-the-way-st-louis-students-are/article_723e3e89-4086-5a9c-8957-f9b8fb654d14.html)

Day Ten
Wednesday August 20th, 2014

Twelve Days in Ferguson, 2014
by Andrew Theising

The artist Fareed Alston documented on video the first twelve days of unrest in Ferguson, from the days after Michael Brown's death to the day of the funeral. He interviewed people at Canfield Green, where the fatal altercation took place; on West Florissant Avenue as protestors held vigils; and at various places around Ferguson, where demonstrators clashed with police at night. Here are some of the words he captured from the people who were there. "Why are you here?" he would ask.

"Justice. That's all we want."
"This [is] history right here."
"It was sad to me."

Some people spoke to the unity they felt.

"It took this dude's life just for everybody to come out today."
"It touches me."
"I feel like I'm part of this."

Some people spoke to the activism.

"I will sleep on the street until I see something done!"
"We came here like so many others, because of what the people of Ferguson have done. They have stood up! Powerfully, courageously, and with persistence, for [nearly] two weeks now."

One person acknowledged that this was about more than what happened in a single place.

"There could be many Fergusons."

Source: (Alston, Fareed. Producer, Director. *Twelve Days in Ferguson*. 40 min. City Productions and Publishing LLC, 2018.) Content used with permission.

Michael Brown and Ferguson

The whole world watched what happened in Ferguson in the weeks following the death of Michael Brown on August 9, 2014. The purpose of this essay is not to contemplate the details of Mr. Brown's case or his death—there are many sources for that analysis—but rather here we will acknowledge the discrimination that occurs throughout history that has brought us to this new chapter in Civil Rights. This experience is as true in the Florissant Valley as it is anywhere. What we saw in Ferguson illustrates the informal (but very real) segregation that continues generations after *Brown v. Board.*

Black Lives Matter

Brown's death was the first killing after the Black Lives Matter movement started, and this timing gave the event a much larger scale than may have been seen in the past. Controversy over the organization parallels the controversy over structural racism and the difficulty our society has in discussing such issues.

The Black Lives Matter movement stemmed from the 2012 killing of 17-year-old Trevon Martin in Florida. The "herstory" (not "history") of the organization begins with three women—Alicia Garza, Patrisse Cullors, and Opal Tometi—who banded together in 2013 to intervene in situations where "Black lives are systematically and intentionally targeted," according to the organization's website. (see https://blacklivesmatter.com /herstory/) Michael Brown's death was the first instance of the group's mobilization. It brought broad attention to the area and transformed the organization into a movement.

"Ferguson was not an aberration," states the herstory, "but…a clear point of reference for what [is] happening in Black communities everywhere." (ibid) It was the organization's involvement in Ferguson that led to its recognition around the world.

Discrimination Continues

There is ample evidence that African Americans experienced direct and indirect discrimination under local, state, and national laws continually since slavery technically was ended in 1865. It continued after the *Brown vs. Board* court decision in 1954. It continued after the Civil Rights Act of 1964. It continued after the Voting Rights Act of 1965, and the Fair Housing Act of 1968, and a seemingly endless stream of court decisions. It is as if each new generation must answer the question anew. It happens today. It has happened in Florissant (see the listing of key court cases stemming from this area for examples).

Housing discrimination, powerfully illustrated in Kenneth Jackson's 1985 book *Crabgrass Frontier*, allowed white persons of means to move out of central cities and forced the poor and persons of color to remain in urban cores amid a crumbling tax base. This is why every American city looks alike today: racially segregated schools and neighborhoods, urban cores dealing with poverty and neglect, and suburbia enjoying stability and wealth.

The Governor of Missouri appointed a commission to study the events that led to Ferguson's unrest and to identify paths toward solutions. The commission issued a report *Forward Through Ferguson* that gives an honest view of the problems and points in the direction of solutions. It is a difficult and challenging path, but a pragmatic one that has realistic steps forward. It is publicly available at www.forwardthrough ferguson.org and is well worth the time to read.

A New Chapter in Civil Rights

What happened in Ferguson was a national reminder that we still have work to do. One notable distinction between the last civil rights movement and the current one is the shift in discussion from "equality" to "equity." As stated above, equality has remained elusive despite the efforts of agencies, legislatures, and courts over the last 50+ years. Equity is proving just as elusive.

The work continues and everyone has a role in it. Corrective action is not the work of others; rather, it involves everyone. The Ferguson Commission has given a straightforward path to define our roles.

A new chapter of America's civil rights story began in the Florissant Valley near the intersection of Chambers Road and West Florissant Avenue. To this end, in some small way, this monograph (and other actions by the Historical Society) helps achieve the Commission's Call to Action around Supporting and Encouraging Creative Spaces. This work is intended to be a tool for relationship-building, awareness, and dialogue. It can be a discussion guide that can inform conversations in classrooms, museums, and faith communities, provided that we are willing to engage in those activities.

Support and Encourage Creative Spaces
Support and encourage spaces with established community presence that think creatively about use-of-space and community relationships to welcome and support casual and professional learning, connecting and dialogue (e.g. City Garden Montessori and other places who are not primarily spaces for this work but will become an important partner in this dialogue). *Accountable body(ies): Diversity, equity, and inclusion practitioners funded by philanthropic community (Forward Through Ferguson: A Path Toward Racial Equity*, p. 160)

Theising image, 2014

FLORISSANT VALLEY QUARTERLY

FLORISSANT VALLEY QUARTERLY

FLORISSANT VALLEY QUARTERLY

CHAPTER THREE

ESSAYS AND ARTICLES FROM THE *QUARTERLY*

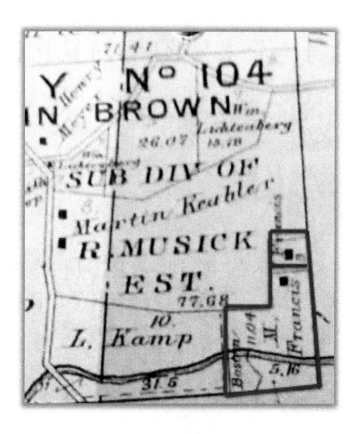

The Francis land is outlined in the lower right corner of this plat map detail, cut from the Musick Estate. Winkler image

Slavery in North County
by Cindy Winkler

Missouri's history is rich and has a significant part in our country's never-ending fascination with the Civil War. As we all have witnessed over the past several years, there is division in this country over war memorials, flags, stories, and the names we choose to keep alive about the Civil War time period and whether it is time to alter the narrative going forward. The Civil War still consumes part of the news cycle after 150+ years. The semi-rural Old Jamestown area (roughly the 63034 ZIP code area today) includes in its history people and circumstances that were deeply affected by the Civil War and slavery. Here is a brief look at the experiences of families at odds, and of two of those people who lived around Old Jamestown: Durrett "Dirk" Patterson, a slaveholder, and Michael Francis, a enslaved person.

Being a slavery state, Missouri was subject to martial law during the war. It was done by order of General John C. Fremont (for whom Florissant's Auguste Archambault had worked on a westward expedition years earlier). The "Provost Marshal" was the chief of the military police units and was responsible for investigating and arresting people on the suspicion of being secessionists. Author Joanne Chiles Eakin wrote a book about these marshals in 1996, called *The Little Gods* to indicate how they behaved.

The Patterson Family came from Virginia and North Carolina to the Florissant Valley, and between them all received land grants and made purchases totaling 2,000 acres along Coldwater Creek. Patterson Road today still joins Old Town Florissant to the old Patterson lands. John Patterson Jr. and his family were among the first Protestants to arrive in the predominantly Catholic valley, arriving in the late 1797. Though the family came from a slavery state, John Patterson was a strong abolitionist.

According to the 1860 Slavery Census, Durrett Patterson owned three enslaved people living in one dwelling. This indicates that the group may have been a family. They were not identified by name, only gender and age: Male, 60 years old; Female, 48 years old; and Female, 18 years old. An 1876 newspaper feature on John Patterson stated that neither he nor his descendants enslaved people "by purchase," but did acknowledge that some descendants received enslaved people through inheritance. Durrett was the grandson of John Patterson, through John's son Elisha.

In July of 1864, Durrett was charged with Violation of the Laws of War and Violation of the Oath of Allegiance he had given in August 1862. He was arrested by order of the Provost Marshal. The charges accused him of passing two letters to John Massey for ultimate conveyance to rebel enemies of the United States. John Massey was Durrett's neighbor (as shown in 1862 and 1878 atlases) and the 1860 Slavery Census shows Massey was a slaveholder as well. Durrett was brought before a Military Commission to review the case against him. The commission ultimately found Durrett not guilty but it does show that some may have had Southern sympathies.

Durrett's older brother, Lewis, also had business with the Provost Marshal. In what could be seen as the complete opposite of his brother's beliefs, Lewis made a sworn statement that another Old Jamestown landowner was a "notorious rebel." Reuben Carrico (son of Daniel and a grandson of Vincent Carrico) was part of a prominent farm family that held enslaved people and owned considerable land along the Missouri River. He, too, had signed an Oath of Allegiance and Lewis's testimony called Reuben's loyalty into question. The statement read, "He expresses himself in every way that a man could against the U.S. Government and also Union men." Reuben was made to pay a fine and re-state his loyalty to the Union. Lewis's pro-Union action and Durrett's accused support for the rebels illustrate how the Civil War truly pitted brother against brother.

A descendant of Durrett Patterson reached out to the author and postulated that Durrett did not make a successful transition from a slaveholder in the post-war Reconstruction period. Durrett survived two decades past the Civil War and stayed in the area. He died in Florissant in 1885 of "inanition"— he starved to death. (He probably lost the ability to swallow or digest.) Ironically, his grandfather's family faced what they called "the starving time" during their migration to the Florissant Valley.

Durrett's place of burial is unknown, but all of his immediate family are buried in Coldwater Cemetery, which was established on Patterson land in the 19th century. It seems logical that he was laid to rest there, too.

A descendant of another Old Jamestown resident also reached out to the author. This woman was the great-granddaughter of Michael Francis, an enslaved person on the Musick estate that was nestled between the Patterson and Carrico land. She had worked diligently on the Francis genealogy and she was able to identify that her ancestors owned land on Old Halls Ferry Road and had been a founder of the New Cold Water Burying Ground. She verified the details of her research with her oldest living relative who confirmed the information.

Depending on relationships and opportunity, some freed enslaved people stayed in the vicinity of their enslavement—even despite strict segregation ordinances that governed their lives as free citizens. There were several communities of African Americans in and around the Florissant Valley.

The Missouri Emancipation Ordinance was authorized on January 11, 1865, and declared forever free all those who had been held in enslavement. Isaac Francis and Michael Francis, perhaps brothers, were among those who survived the experience and were granted freedom. Lydia Carrico Musick, who had grown up on the Vincent Carrico estate (with her brother Daniel) and married Reuben Musick (owner of Musick's Ferry), gave the two Francis men plots of land to call their own. She had inherited parts of her father's land and gave these acres to Isaac and Michael. This land was near Cold Water Creek and Old Halls Ferry Road. *[It may be that Isaac Francis is actually Isaac Thomas, who was Michael's father. Records are unclear.]*

Isaac and his wife remained servants and friends of Reuben Musick until his death in 1871, as documents pertaining to the settlement of his estate would seem to indicate. Specifically, in an affidavit relating to the estate of Reuben Musick dated March of 1872, Emma Broughton, a neighbor of the Musicks, set forth how Isaac and his wife cared for Reuben in his last days, including difficult wound treatment and the furnishing and preparation of provisions for all of the company that came in Mr. Musick's last days.

Michael Francis died in 1913 from tuberculosis. He is buried at the New Coldwater Burial Ground that he helped create.

(originally published with Andrew Theising as "Slavery in the Florissant Valley," *Florissant Valley Quarterly* October 2019)

Mr. Doss holding a souvenir stein during his visit to Taille de Noyer in 1988.   Theising photo

The View from the Servants' House
by Andrew Theising

The weather was unpleasant, so only a few interested souls braved it to Taille de Noyer for a tour. I was chatting with Mrs. Jane Millick, a new member of the Society, when a man peered through the window and tapped on the glass. The man was Lewis L. Doss Sr., and he was returning to the house for the first time since 1950.

I was fascinated with him from the moment he entered the house. He had worked for Julius and Sarah Polk, the last residents of Taille. "My mother was the cook," remarked Mr. Doss, "and my grandmother worked here, too." Mr. Doss had not known of the events of the house since the Historical Society acquired it. Both Jane and I went with Mr. Doss and he recollected the days when Taille de Noyer was home to the last of Florissant's old aristocracy.

Mr. Doss remembered the many grandchildren who would visit. "We had to break up the little fights," he said with a smile. "They were cute kids – beautiful kids." As he looked out through the large door in the log portion of the house, he recalled the fields that once graced the property. "There were wheat fields from the edge of the yard to the Florissant Road. On the side of the house was the best of gardens. Mrs. Polk had a compost patch there. We would throw out the seed and you could almost see it growing!"

The window in the door of the dog trot area has a wood with "drop" door that will lock to cover the glass panes. Mr. Doss recalled that the Polks would tell of that window being used to watch for Indians in the early days of the house. He said he knew that the rooms were log, but had never seen them exposed as they are today.

As he walked into the dining room, he remembered the parties that the Polks would have at Taille. He said that Mrs. Polk loved to entertain, and that she did so often. "Every Monday, the ladies would meet to play bridge. They would get into groups and spread out across the house. We would serve them sherry and cake, a brown cake with raisins. She was an entertainer!"

As we went into the kitchen, he remembered his mother, who now lives with him in Wisconsin. "My mother was an excellent cook. I can remember enjoying some fish that my mother would bake. She would add bay leaf and lemon juice. I don't remember what kind of fish it was, but I would clean the platter after the table was cleared. I will never forget that!" As we looked around, he explained that the servants' house was a three-bedroom structure that stood directly behind the kitchen. "It was blue. My mother would stand in the kitchen and look straight into the window of our house. That's how she would watch us kids. If we were fighting, she could run right out the back door and stop us. She could see right into our window."

As we went to the second floor, Mr. Doss remembered the large plank floors, remarking that they were painted then just like they are today. He said that the display room today really looked like Mr. Polk's room. "Mr. Polk ran an antique shop downtown. He had some beautiful pieces of furniture. I would get to ride down there with him. He would drop me off to do a job downtown, and he would go to his shop. He kept his stock on a porch at Taille under a tarp. It was beautiful. Mrs. Polk gave me a leather chair with animals carved into the handles. I treasure that chair. I gave it to my grandmother to use. I don't know whatever happened to it."

I asked Mr. Doss where he used to go shopping. "I don't think I ever saw Florissant. It is not familiar to me. We used to go to Ferguson to shop. We bought everything there. I don't remember the names, but my mother would. I later worked at Shear's department store in Ferguson. I never saw Florissant."

"Mr. Polk's son was called 'Polkey,'" he remarked. Polkey had one of the rooms upstairs. As we left the master bedroom on the second floor, Mr. Doss remarked "this is Mrs. Polk's room. I am sure of it. We could see her through this window. She was always doing something with her hands. She was a fantastic seamstress."

"Mrs. Polk was something else. She had a proud walk, and was a youthful woman. She was in her 60s when I was last here but you would never know it. She was a classy lady — beautiful. She was the counselor of the family. There was a phone in the hallway outside of the kitchen. You couldn't help but hear her counseling one of her daughters. They all related to their mother."

Mr. Doss never had occasion to see the third floor of Taille. "I don't know what this would have been used for. I am sure it was for storage. Mrs. Polk might have kept her sewing things here. She did her sewing on the first floor, but I never saw where she kept it," he said.

We went to the lower level of the house next. It was not added to Taille until the Society acquired the property. "All that was here was a small cellar. We used to store flower bulbs and plants there. Dahlias, flags, tulips, parsnip roots – all kinds."

"There was a lot of work in the spring. She always had work. There were so many shrubs that had to be cared for. There were shrubs and beautiful flowers all around. It was a little paradise. It was just beautiful."

I asked Mr. Doss about other buildings that used to stand at the house. His mother's house (the servants' house) was directly behind the kitchen. Mr. Doss continued: "there was another house for the caretaker of the yards. He was responsible for all of the gardens, but I still had to go out and cut the vines and things that would grow in the shrubs.

There were two very old barns that stood nearby. I remember the square nails. I think they were demolished while I was still here. Mrs. Polk's horse was named Pegasus. We would take the grandkids to the old barn and let them ride the horse and so would we. He once threw me. I don't remember exactly, but I wound up on the ground!"

"There was a spring a short ride from here. It was down a hill and I remember that there was a hole under an embankment. Water would flow out — cool, good and fresh. We would ride down there. You couldn't swim in it, but we would stop by for water when we were out that way," he said.

"My job was keeping the cars cleaned and washed. Mrs. Polk had a huge car, a Lincoln Zephyr. It was an old car and she wanted it to shine. Mr. Polk drove a Hudson, and it had a big trunk. That was also a nice car. I had to keep them clean," he remembered.

Mr. Doss said his mother worked here first. There are six brothers in his family, four of them were here while the family was at Taille. His grandmother came north from Mississippi and also came to work for the Polks. In addition to this, his other grandmother worked for one of the Polk daughters, Grizelda, who lived on Newstead Avenue.

"My grandmother wanted a place of her own, so she bought a place in Kinloch. We bought a Quonset hut from somebody in the city. It was 16x16 and we had it hauled all the way from Jefferson Barracks. Mrs. Polk let us erect it behind my mother's house. My brother and I lived there."

Mr. Doss recalled sweeping the long porch on the front of the house, and how he enjoyed living out here. "We created our own lifestyle here. In those days, you made the most with what you had. We did, and we loved it!"

All the while he was touring the house, Mr. Doss kept saying what a treat this was for him. Believe me, Mr. Doss, the pleasure was all mine. Welcome back!

Mr. Doss shared a recipe for "ginger pears" with us. Take pears that have been sectioned and smother them in sugar. Let them sit overnight so that the sugar can draw out the juices from the pears. Add to this some lemon juice, ginger root, and cinnamon bark. Cook them until they are tender – the sugar makes a delicious syrup. Mr. Doss assured me they're quite good.

(originally published as "A Visit to Taille de Noyer," *Florissant Valley Quarterly*, April 1988)

Taille de Noyer as it appeared in the 1940s, when Mr. Doss and his family worked there. Library of Congress

Mr. Doss's family mentioned in this story:

- His mother, who worked at Taille de Noyer, was **Mary A. Barr** (1912-2002).
- His younger brother was **Linton Doss**, who died at age 43 (1933-1976).
- His maternal grandmother, who bought a house in Kinloch, was **Lela Belle Curtis** (1890-1977).
- His paternal grandmother, who worked for Grizelda Gilchrist (Polk) Skinner, was **Katie Doss** (born 1891).
- **Lewis Lemar Doss Sr.** himself was born in 1932 and died in 2001. He was 69 years old. He was a veteran of the Korean War (Corporal, U. S. Army) and is buried at the Southern Wisconsin Veterans Memorial Cemetery near Racine, Wisconsin.
- He was married 48 years to his wife, **Hettie I. (Jones) Doss**. They were the parents of 11 children, had 34 grandchildren, and three great-grandchildren.
- His son, the **Rev. Lewis Lemar Doss Jr.**, was born in 1958 and died in 2010, at age 52.

While we have no further details of Mr. Doss's family members, it is striking that three of the seven passed away at younger ages. Reduced life expectancy is yet another tragic legacy of slavery and racism that exists today.

Attempting to Heal the Slavery
at St. Stanislaus

When the first Jesuits came to Florissant in 1823, six enslaved people accompanied the priests. They were identified as Thomas and Mary (Molly/Polly) Brown, Moses and Nancy Queen, and Isaac and Susan Queen-Hawkins. In 1829, two more families were forced to relocate from Maryland to Florissant to serve the Jesuits, also bearing the Hawkins and Queen surnames. A total of 22 enslaved people (adults and children) then resided on the St. Stanislaus property.

The Jesuits of Central and Southern USA, which serves Missouri, have launched the "Slavery, History, Memory, and Reconciliation Project" to help trace the Jesuit role in slavery in the United States and locate descendants of enslaved families.

The Jesuits operated a plantation at White Marsh, Maryland, since 1729 that depended on enslaved labor and indentured servitude. St. Stanislaus Seminary in Florissant was established from the White Marsh facility.

The *Quarterly* is featuring articles and notes to coincide with the "1619 Project" that recognized British slavery's 400th anniversary. Last issue's article by Cindy Winkler was well received and we will continue this topic for the next few issues.

The original publication included a map from 1836, not included here, showing the location of "Cabins for Negroes" on Howdershell Road. The map indicated that the cabins stood near the entrance drive of the property at 700 Howdershell Road. (Note—two cabins were shown for 22 known people!)

(Originally published as "Jesuits Search for Slave Descendants" in the January 2020 *Florissant Valley Quarterly*.)

Above: The "Rock" Building at St. Stanislaus Seminary in the 1930s, built by enslaved people. Library of Congress Image.

Below: St. Ferdinand's Church as it appeared from the 1840s to the 1870s, after the rectory wing was added to the left of the sanctuary. Nicholas Point S.J. was the artist. Davison/Washington State Image

Places of Worship for Enslaved People in Florissant

Based on a small part of Kelly L. Schmidt's article, "Enslaved Faith Communities in the Jesuits' Missouri Mission," U.S. Catholic Historian Journal; Vol. 37, No. 2, Spring 2019, pp. 49-82. Ms. Schmidt's full article is a deep and thoughtful essay that covers much more than this excerpt.

When the Jesuits arrived in Florissant in 1823, they brought six enslaved people with them from Maryland. These bonded workers took up their residence at the St. Stanislaus Seminary complex on Howdershell Road. Though the Jesuits ministered to the enslaved people, this was done separately from ministry to whites in most cases. Between 1823 and 1849, there were two places where enslaved people worshipped and received sacraments: St. Ferdinand's Church and in the Jesuit chapel at St. Stanislaus. Ms. Schmidt notes that there was very little ministry in secular places (such as homes), except where a birth or death may be occurring and requiring immediate rites. There is sufficient evidence in the St. Ferdinand Church records to show that enslaved people played a role in the life of the parish. It is probable that the rear pews of the sanctuary were reserved for their use during these earliest years.

Segregated space for worship began in earnest in the 1840s. Early in that decade, the addition of the rectory wing to St. Ferdinand's was completed and added space with a side view of the altar. This new space became the seating area for the enslaved, and could be accessed by entering the building from the rear rather than the front doors. It also gave them an opportunity for more direct interaction with the enslaved of local parishioners and the Sisters who lived there over the years. By the end of that decade, the Jesuits had completed what is today the "Old Rock Building," which allowed them to vacate the early log/frame structure and dedicate the second floor of it to be a "chapel for the Negroes." (It should be noted that this log structure and the rock building were built with enslaved labor.)

The chapel space served both enslaved and free persons of color. The preaching was done not by ordained priests, but rather by novices, scholastics, and brothers in the Jesuit order. It probably diminished the enslaved people's presence at Saint Ferdinand's and certainly reduced the workload of the pastor there, who at times had made the two-mile walk to St. Stanislaus to hear confessions and minister to the enslaved— "likely so that the walk to Saint Ferdinand would not diminish their work hours."

(Originally published as "Jesuits Search for Slave Descendants" in the April 2020 edition of the *Florissant Valley Quarterly*.)

Left, Upper: The original buildings of St. Stanislaus were built of log, using the labor of enslaved people. Once the "Rock" building was completed, the log chapel was used for African American worshippers. Library of Congress Image

Left, Lower: Aerial view of St. Stanislaus Seminary complex, circa 1930s. The white stone "Rock" building with its tall cupola stands just left of center. The old cabins for enslaved people (where Peter Hawkins would have lived as a child) stood just off the bottom right edge of the photo at the entrance on Howdershell Road. The road winds through the trees from the upper left. Library of Congress Image

Peter Hawkins and the Enslaved Community of St. Stanislaus

by Kelly L. Schmidt, Research Coordinator,
Jesuit Slavery, History, Memory, and Reconciliation Project

Peter Hawkins was the first child born into slavery at the Jesuits' Saint Stanislaus Novitiate and Farm in Florissant, Missouri, and the last formerly-enslaved person to leave the seminary after emancipation. He witnessed and lived through almost the entirety of enslaved people's presence at Saint Stanislaus. As an adult, his wisdom, experience, and devotion to the Catholic faith led several Black Catholics in the Florissant Valley area to choose him as their godfather at baptisms and as witness at their marriages.

Peter's parents, Isaac Hawkins and Susanna (often called Susan, or Succy) Queen, were newlyweds of only four months when they were forced along with two other enslaved couples to aid in founding the Jesuits' new Missouri mission. In May 1823 they endured a month-long journey of over a thousand miles by foot and flatboat along the Ohio River from the Jesuits' plantation in White Marsh, Maryland, to Florissant, Missouri. Isaac frequently navigated the flotilla out of trouble when caught in a current, and steered the boats at night. After arriving in Florissant, Isaac and Susan settled into a crowded, one-room log cabin that doubled as the kitchen and laundry, which they shared with the other two enslaved families. Isaac and Susan Hawkins, Thomas and Molly Brown, and Moses and Nancy Queen were forced to commence the difficult work of constructing the novitiate's new buildings, farming, and sewing, laundering, and cooking for the Jesuits.

On May 8, 1824, Susan Hawkins gave birth to Peter in their crowded cabin. Peter was baptized conditionally the day of his birth because he was in danger of death. The full ceremonies were performed in June. Records show that Peter and Susan remained sickly over the following years. At age twenty, again in danger of death, Peter received the Catholic sacrament of anointing of the sick. Peter's brother, William, born in April 1834, lived only six months.

Through births, purchases, and the transfer of two more families from the White Marsh plantation in Maryland—including some of Peter's relatives—the enslaved community at Saint Stanislaus grew from seven to about 35 people during Peter Hawkins' lifetime. After the Jesuits became administrators of Saint Louis College (now Saint Louis University), several of Peter's kin were sent to labor at the college. Many enslaved people were transferred back and forth to labor between the Florissant farm at Saint Stanislaus, the downtown university, and the College Farm north of the city over the following years.

Peter and his kin built relationships with and became influential among the enslaved and free African American communities in the Florissant Valley. Enslaved people visited one another across plantations and properties in evening hours. They took advantage of feast days and mass attendance at Saint Ferdinand Church to gather together.

They sold produce from their own garden plots and worked extra hours at night for pay to obtain funds to make their own purchases or to buy their freedom. Many bondspeople used some of the money to buy better-quality materials than what the Jesuits supplied, so that when they gathered with kin for services, they could show off their finest clothing. People of color gradually began building shanties in the woods near Saint Stanislaus in order to be nearer to the Jesuits' enslaved community, and to join them in attending religious services at the chapel later designated on the property for enslaved people.

With his kin community, Peter experienced the brutality of enslavement at the hands of his Jesuit masters, and participated with fellow bondspeople in resisting their treatment. Peter may have watched as Jesuits prepared to have an enslaved man flogged, until the man's wife rescued him by throwing herself in front of the whip and flinging her arms around her husband. This couple could very well have been Peter's own parents. Peter may have been present on another occasion when enslaved women prevented another person's beating by picking up rocks to hurl at the inflictor. Peter was only about eight years old when, because a woman refused to remove her own clothing to be whipped, the Jesuit superior ordered a layman to strip and tie her, calling Jesuits to view the whipping as the woman's sister cried out, "My sister is naked!" Peter was also severed from relatives and loved ones when Jesuits sold them away as punishment.

Jesuits lauded Peter Hawkins for his religious piety and for being "the best slave," but Peter's faith did not stop him from resisting his enslavement to the Jesuits and pursuing freedom. In fact, he leveraged his perceived devotion as a strategy to negotiate with the Jesuits toward his own goals. He arranged with the Jesuits to allow him to work for hire in Florissant and Saint Louis to begin buying his freedom. Later, in 1862, Peter convinced the Jesuits to purchase a woman named Margaret, whom he wished to marry, from Charles G. McHatton, to prevent them from being separated. Jesuits agreed to this purchase as a supposed "reward" for Peter's loyalty, but stipulated that Peter, by his own labor, must pay them the $800 price for Margaret's purchase before the couple could be free.

For two years after marrying Margaret, Peter labored day and night to earn the funds for their freedom. Still, he could not make enough to pay off Margaret's purchase price—an estimated equivalent of $20,308.04 today— from the meager tips he received from being hired out. In May 1864, Peter came to the Jesuits demanding that the price they were asking him to pay for his and Margaret's freedom was too much. The Jesuits, in turn, grumbled that Peter must have been prodded on by fellow bondspeople to have become so dissatisfied. Many were already running away or expressing their discontent. They complained, "Peter, a Black slave in our house of Probation [Novitiate], like almost all the other slaves these days, who have gone giddy, wants to leave us and live of his own right. But he had promised to repay us the money that we spent to buy his wife two years ago."

Peter's persistence forced the Jesuits to compromise. The consultors agreed to absolve half of Margaret's $800 purchase price. They gave Peter a choice about how he would pay the remaining $400: he and Margaret could either take whatever possessions they had and go live as free people, paying the remainder over time, or, Peter could remain laboring for the Jesuits on their property for another two years, after which he and Margaret could then leave as free people without financial obligation. Peter and Margaret chose to stay.

Less than one year into this agreement, Missouri legislators abolished slavery on January 11, 1865. Yet Peter and Margaret continued to labor without compensation for two more years. Several days after the abolition legislation, Missouri Jesuits had decided to make contracts "with regard to pay" with all other remaining free people to continue working on the Jesuits' farm for a salary. However they held Peter and Margaret in a state of debt peonage (debt slavery), as they continued to labor unrecompensed to pay off the imposed debt for Margaret's purchase. In 1866, Peter requested that the Jesuits grant him a ten-acre plot of farmland on which he could live and work. The Jesuits said no—they claimed it would be inefficient. Peter did not receive a salary until January 15, 1867, two years after the abolition of slavery. Peter's wages were $14.00 per month; Margaret's, $5.00 per month.

Debt peonage and low wages were just a few of the tactics used by former slaveholders, including the Jesuits, to oppress Black Americans immediately after the abolition of slavery. Such practices did not end in the years following the Civil War and Reconstruction. From the Jim Crow era until today, as their oppressors have continued to find new ways to perpetuate structural violence and systemic racism—voter suppression, housing discrimination, mass incarceration, to name only a few— Black Americans have continued to struggle for civil and human rights. The struggle to achieve racial justice and dismantle white supremacy continues today, including in the mass protests that have emerged in response to ongoing police brutality throughout the United States.

Despite everything he endured, Peter remained with the Jesuits until about the time of his death in 1907, having spent his entire life in service to the Jesuits even though they had so mistreated him. Perhaps Peter and Margaret remained at Saint Stanislaus so they could continue to be near the close kin community they had known for most of their lives. Peter and Margaret Hawkins had become central figures in the enslaved and free African American community around Florissant. As sponsors at baptisms while in bondage and after freedom, they continued to draw members of their community together, building stability in the uncertain aftermath of slavery.

Peter Hawkins was one of many people held in bondage by the Society of Jesus who resiliently shaped their own cultures and communities as they resisted their enslavement. For more about them, visit shmr.jesuits.org.

(Originally published in the July 2020 *Quarterly*. The accompanying image, used with permission, officially is titled Image of Peter Hawkins, MIS Box 2.0215, Album 25. Missouri Province Scrapbook/Album collection, Jesuit Archives & Research Center, St. Louis, Missouri.)

Peter Hawkins, about 1905. Courtesy of the Jesuit Archives & Research Center

Lucy Delaney's Triumphant Pursuit of Freedom

by Andrew Theising

The concluding essay in our yearlong examination of slavery in Florissant

Lucy Ann Delaney was born into slavery in St. Louis in 1824. Her father is not named, but he was taken from the family and sold in Vicksburg MS. Her mother was Polly Crockett (a.k.a. Polly Wash), an enslaved woman who technically was free living in Illinois, then taken in her youth and sold back into slavery in Missouri.

Lucy was born on the estate of Major Taylor Berry, who was a very unusual character. He had been a founding father of Columbia MO and was a prominent veteran of the War of 1812. He was accused of forgery and perjury in 1824, was arrested, and was tried for the crimes. The jury acquitted him, but he felt public humiliation over the trial. He sought his revenge against the prosecutor, attorney Abiel Leonard, and attacked Leonard repeatedly with a rawhide whip. Leonard fought back and challenged Berry to a duel, which led to Berry's death. His enslaved workers were not freed, so Lucy, her sister Nancy, and her mother Polly remained enslaved by the family. Lucy was sent to live in another household. In their desperation, Polly and Nancy escaped.

Nancy fled to Canada. Polly made it to Chicago but was caught and returned to jail in St. Louis. Lucy (now 12 years old) remained in slavery and was returned to the Berry family's household to fill Nancy's role. (2)

The household was that of Mary Berry Coxe and Henry Coxe. It was an abusive relationship and household. Their children died in infancy. Henry was a drunkard. Mary was prone to outbursts of anger. Both of them had fierce personalities.

Technically, her new owner, James Magehan, committed Polly to the County jail and while there, her services were "rented" out. She was "hired" by Elijah Haydon, a St. Louisan who gave her great freedom of movement and association. (4) Polly became connected with Harris Sproat, an attorney who occasionally had taken on African American clients. She sued for her freedom on October 3, 1839. (4) It was a long and drawn-out process.

In the meantime, Mary gave Lucy as a wedding present to her sister Martha Mitchell (Mrs. David D. Mitchell). Martha was not located far from the Haydon home. Lucy's job for Martha was as a laundress—a back-breaking job that may have meant hauling 50 gallons of water for every load, working over open fires, and scrubbing clothes using lye and bare hands. She was inexperienced. Martha also had a fiery temper (modern reviewers of the record have suggested she was manic-depressive) and yelled her complaints at Lucy. Lucy fired back, "You don't know nothing yourself about it" and told her to "get someone to teach me." Martha threatened Lucy with physical punishment. Lucy exclaimed, "You have no business to whip me; I don't belong to you." With that, Lucy fled out the front door in terror, ran to her mother's location, and hid away dreaming that her hiding space was "a boat [that] was steaming down South." (4)

The battle had begun. Polly had a "next friend" suit filed (one of the few ways an enslaved person could file a suit) by a sympathetic attorney with the intent of gaining some kind of possession of her daughter on September 8, 1842. In doing so, Lucy was taken from her hiding place to the county jail by the Sheriff. Both Mr. Mitchell (Lucy's present owner and the respondent of the suit) and his brother-in-law Mr. Coxe (Lucy's previous owner) met her at the jail. The presiding judge was Bryan Mullanphy, son of John Mullanphy and brother of Jane Chambers who resided at Taille de Noyer. (4) He was an eccentric man who had lived in Florissant for a time and had a genuine concern for the plight of the poor.

Polly's case finally moved to trial on June 6, 1843. Polly's case also was on Judge Mullanphy's docket before a jury of 12 white men. Attorney Sproat made a simple argument: Polly had been taken to Illinois in her youth by Joseph Crockett for a period longer than 60 days and was never registered there as an enslaved person. Therefore she was free under Illinois law, and her subsequent sales to Taylor Berry, Mary Berry Coxe, and Joseph Magehan were improper. "Once free ... always free." Astonishingly, the jury agreed and Judge Mullanphy ordered her freedom. (4) Now Polly focused on her daughter.

Polly engaged two attorneys to help her daughter. The first was Francis Butter Murdoch, one of St. Louis's most prominent freedom-suit lawyers. The second was Edward Bates, of Florissant, a legal powerhouse who had been the prosecutor under Territorial Governor William Clark and who would go on to become Lincoln's Attorney General during the Civil War. His interest in the case is peculiar, being a slaveholder himself who had defended owners during such suits. (4) It seems that he liked the drama of it and loved a public oratory on a powerful subject.

When Lucy's case was finally heard in Judge Mullanphy's courtroom in 1844, Bates took center stage. He relied heavily on the legal precedent established in Polly's case: once free, always free. He drew in the jurors with his emphatic style and legal logic. He recounted Polly's story, her struggles and treatment *as a free woman*. Bates got the Berry family to testify that Lucy was indeed Polly's child, since no documentation existed. He concluded with powerful words that won the jury over to his side: "Gentlemen of the jury, I am a slaveholder myself, but, thanks to Almighty God, I am above the base principle of holding anybody a slave that has as good a right to her freedom as this girl has been proven to have; she was free before she was born; her mother was free, but kidnapped in her youth, and sacrificed to the greed of negro traders, and no free woman can give birth to a slave child, as it is direct violation to the laws of God and man!" (4) The jury was convinced and found her to be a free woman. Lucy was ecstatic and cried tears of joy at the news, praising Bates and Mullanphy.

Mitchell's lawyer was outraged and demanded Lucy be sent back to jail while he appealed, claiming he did "not consider that the case has had a fair trial." (4) Bates jumped to his feet and retorted: "For shame! Is it not enough that this girl has been deprived of her liberty for a year and a half, that you must still pursue her after a fair and impartial trial before jury? I demand that she be set at liberty at once." (4) Judge Mullanphy took advantage of the moment, ignored the complaints from Mitchell, and set Lucy free there and then.

Lucy recounted her story in a book almost fifty years later, *From the Darkness Cometh the Light, or Struggles for Freedom* (St. Louis: J. T. Smith, 1891). She did reunite with her father, if only briefly, and moved eventually to Quincy IL. She married Frederick Turner. Tragically, he was killed in an explosion aboard a steamship. In great irony, that ship was named the *Edward Bates*.

Notes and Sources:
1. Missouri Digital Heritage. "A Brief Biography of Abiel Leonard," <u>Crack of the Pistol</u>.
2. "Lucy A. Delaney," <u>Documenting the American South</u>.
3. "Lucy A. Delaney," <u>Oxford Reference.</u>
4. "You Have No Business to Whip Me," <u>African American Review</u>. Spring 2007.

(Originally published in the October 2020 *Quarterly*.)

For a thoughtful documentation of freedom trials like Ms. Delaney's, visit the Washington University archives for digital images from actual St. Louis court cases, including the Squire Brown case at: http://repository.wustl.edu/concern/ texts/kp78gh84b. You can also search for "Squire Brown" online and find interesting documents.

Also, read the accounts documented and analyzed thoroughly by Dale Edwyna Smith in *African American Lives in St. Louis 1763-1865* (Jefferson NC: McFarland and Co. Publishers, 2017).

The New Coldwater Burying Ground: Preserving an African American Cemetery

By the St. Angela Merici School 7th Graders of 1976

[Editor's Note: This was published originally in July 1976 as "A Brief History of the Cemetery Written by the Seventh Grade," in the old run of the Quarterly *before its present series. St. Angela Merici School Boy Scouts, as part of a Bicentennial service project, worked at the cemetery and 7th graders researched and wrote the piece. The article is reproduced here partially and edited, with different imagery and addendum to clarify the historical record.]*

Rededication Ceremony, May 23, 1976

During our months of research on the cemetery project, we have interviewed many people. They were full of information, but still there is more needed. Now, we will briefly summarize what we have found out.

The deed told us that the cemetery was purchased in 1886, on the 27th day of September, for $50.00. This money was gathered by Henry Vincent, who went around the community to collect it. This deed was between sellers Frederick W. Tyler, May E. and David Benton, Mario O. and James G. Harris, Anna W. and George W. Hume, all of the county of St. Louis; and buyers **Henry Vincent**, **Louis Gassaway**, **William Cooper**, **Mike Francis**, and **William Brooks**. The cemetery is now under the name of the "New Coldwater Burying Grounds."

The cemetery occupies one-half acre of land. The tiny area had been taken over by weeds and thorn bushes until everybody started working. But long before the current community project, a 77-year-old man named Frazier Vincent had attempted to fix it up. Frazier Vincent's parents were enslaved, and both of them are buried in the cemetery. His father, Henry Vincent, helped collect the $50 needed to buy the cemetery as said earlier. Henry Vincent died in 1900 and Delia Vincent died in 1909. Out of Frazier's five siblings, two brothers are buried in the cemetery. Both died in 1949.

Another family attending the ceremony today is the Cambrons. Lucille Cambron's family lived in this area since the Civil War. Her great-grandmother was **Helen Green**, who married **Charlie Pope**. They had seven children: **Susan, Helen, Letishia, John, Charlie, Lizzie, and Julia**. Lizzie married a **Campbell**, John married a woman named **Lilly**, and Letishia married **Wallace Phoenix**. Lucille is here at the ceremony today as a representative of the 33 people buried in the cemetery.

Since the cemetery held Frazier Vincent's family and friends, he labored for a month cleaning the cemetery, with only the help of a pair of hand cutters and a tiny saw. Many people admired his work, but in a few years it was again overgrown. It is now the goal of the community to fulfill Frazier Vincent's dreams (as well as those of the other workers of the past) of getting rid of all the overgrowth in the tiny area and to have other people care enough to keep it in good condition.

We hope that our example will cause people to stop and want to take care of something when it needs to be cared for. If this is done, when somebody says: "Missouri is the Show-Me State, so show me," we won't have to look any farther than our own hearts to find something to be proud of, just as we, the community members, are proud of this cemetery.

Addendum:

Frazier Vincent Sr. was the son of **Delia Hayes** (1848-1909) and **Henry Vincent** (1831-1900), two of the formerly enslaved people who established the new Coldwater Burying Ground in 1886. In an old *Florissant Valley Reporter* article from 1959, preserved by Peggy Kruse in her book *Old Jamestown Across the Ages*, Frazier Vincent recalled the building that stood adjacent to the cemetery that was a church on Sunday and a school other days of the week. "We had a preacher mostly every Sunday," he recalled, and the service would be followed by a lunch outside under the large old trees.

The Vincent family worked as farmers on the Desloge family estate (not far from the Musick's Ferry settlement) and later rented farmland near New Halls Ferry and Shackelford Roads, where they stayed for 14 years. Frazier Vincent Sr. was the last interment at the New Coldwater Burying Ground.

Addendum source: Kruse, Peggy. *Old Jamestown Across the Ages.* Revised edition. St. Louis: Peace Weavers LLC, 2018. Pp. 182-183.
The FindAGrave website is remarkably complete for Mr. Vincent. See memorial #195374995.

Rededication of the

NEW COLDWATER BURYING GROUNDS

Sunday, May 23, 1976

1:30 P.M.

Program cover from the 1976 Re-dedication. FVHS Image

Above: Lucille Cambron and other family members at the 1976 rededication of the New Coldwater Burying Ground. FVHS Image

Below: Frazier Vincent, the last trustee of the cemetery, was the final burial in New Coldwater. Gladbach photo.

COMPENDIUM
A Collection of Facts, Ephemera, and Stories

The Barnabas Harris Estate

This estate sale advertisement from the *Missouri Gazette*, December 15, 1819, is among the earliest newspaper mentions of Florissant to be found. It is unclear where the Barnabas Harris estate "near Florissant" was exactly. He was an early Missouri Territory political figure. However, note that the estate consists of eight enslaved people.

Public Sale.

WILL be sold on Saturday the 8th day of January next, at the house of Barnabi Harris, deceased, near Florisant, between 1000 and 1500 bushels of Corn, And a small light Waggon, Terms of sale will be nine months credi, the purchaser giving bond with approved security

Will be hired at the same time, for the term of one year, a plantation of about 40 acres, with good cabbins, eight Negroes consisting of men, women and children.

Frederick Hyatt, Admin'r.
December 15th, 1819.   3t85

(Originally published in the Miscellany section of the April 2020 edition of the *Florissant Valley Quarterly*)

From the Gilbert Garraghan History
St. Ferdinand de Florissant (1923)

There is an 1813 record cited in Garraghan (page 149) that "**Philip**, a negro," and "**Marianne**, a negress," each offered St. Ferdinand's Church as a donation a *carrotte* of tobacco, a recognized medium of exchange under the Spanish regime, rated as the equivalent of 40 cents. It is a carrot-shaped mass of compressed tobacco.

1817 Labor Rates

Thomas Scharf, in his 1883 *History of St. Louis City and County* (page 1287) cites the labor rates that appeared in the November 1817 *Missouri Gazette*:
- Bricklayers, masons, carpenters: $3 per day
- White laborers: $1.50 per day
- Negro laborers: $18-$25 per month
- Enslaved females hired out: $5 to $15 per month.

A Glimpse of Married Life for the Enslaved

The *WPA Slave Narratives (Missouri)* from the Library of Congress are priceless resources of memory. Among many other topics, they give an idea of what married life would have been like for some enslaved people. One woman, **Mary A. Bell**, daughter of the prominent preacher **Spottswood Rice**, described married life for her parents. She was interviewed in St. Louis County in 1936, but her family worked in rural Missouri (unidentified, but probably closer to Kansas City).

"...My father was not allowed to come to see my mother but two nights a week. That was Wednesday and Saturday. So often he came home all bloody from beatings his old overseer would give him. My mother would take those bloody clothes off him, bathe the sore places, and grease them good; and wash and iron his clothes so he could go back clean."

"…Once he came home bloody after a beating he did not deserve and he ran away. He scared my mother almost to death because he had run away, and she did all in her power to persuade him to go back. He said he would die first, so he hid three days and three nights, under houses and in the woods, looking for a chance to cross the line but the patrollers were so hot on his trail he couldn't make it."

"After three days and three nights he was so weak and hungry that he came out and gave himself up to a slave-trader that he knew, and begged the trader to buy him from his owner, Mr. Lewis, because Mr. Lewis was so mean to him." The trader did not do so, said that Mr. Lewis's farm would be ruined without him [Mr. Rice was the equivalent of a foreman and was quite effective in the role], but encouraged him to settle his dispute with Mr. Lewis, which he did.

Mary Bell reported that she was rented to a minister's family and later to another family starting at the age of 7. She would assist with childcare, collect food, and deliver communication to workers in the fields. In this case, husband, wife, and at least one child were all at separate locations.

Mr. Rice left the farm where he worked, took six of the best men with him, and all joined the Union Army at Kansas City. When the farmer balked and demanded their return, the Army informed him that they were soldiers now and would not be returning to his farm.

(Source: see the typewritten manuscript available on the Library of Congress website, therein noted as page 6, with the odd heading "She Loves Army Men" referring to her love for the veterans in her immediate family.) Available from www.loc.gov/item/mesn100/.

The Story of Mattie J. Jackson

There is another narrative of a formerly enslaved person that may be of interest to people researching North County. **Mattie Jackson** (1847-1910) dictated her story to Dr. L. S. Thompson, who then edited and published Ms. Jackson's story in 1866.

While there is no concrete connection to the Florissant Valley, her enslaved family was brought to Missouri from the East Coast. In Missouri, they were taken from St. Charles to Bremen (now approximately the Hyde Park neighborhood in North St. Louis). This path would essentially follow Natural Bridge Road through the southern part of the township.

She reports slaveholders with the names Harris and Lewis, and enslaved persons with the names Jackson and Turner—all surnames recorded in the St. Ferdinand Township records. She even mentions General Daniel Marsh Frost (inheritor of Hazelwood Farm) in passing.

Her book is another story of slaveholders, traders, jails, and family separation. Of particular historical interest is her discussion of being held by Bernard Lynch ("Linch") in his infamous slave-pens in downtown St. Louis.

Source: Thompson, Dr. L. S. *The Story of Mattie J. Jackson.* Lawrence MA: The Sentinal, 1866. Available through UNC Chapel Hill <docsouth.unc.edu> and also Gutenberg.org.

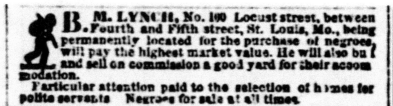

Advertisement for the notorious Bernard M. Lynch, 1859. Mattie Jackson was kept there during her ordeal being enslaved. The pens were atrocious, yet are advertised as "a good yard" for "accommodation." Newspapers.com

Mary Armstrong, here in 1936 at age 91, was born into slavery in St. Louis about 1845. "Old Satan in torment," she said, "couldn't be no meaner than [her St. Louis owners] was to they slaves." WPA Slave Narratives (Texas), Library of Congress

Michael Powers Real Estate

This advertisement was from 1859 by Michael Powers, who owned and sold a considerable amount of land in Old Town Florissant. Here he offers undefined plots of land, including his own home that was fit with a smoke house, a carriage house, and "negro quarters."

FLORISSANT TOWN PROPERTY.

I HAVE several blocks of ground three hundred feet square, in the city of St. Ferdinand, among which are some beautiful building sites. To any person who will improve them, good bargains will be given, and the terms will be unusually liberal. On the premises for sale are two young orchards of all kinds of fruit. Or, with a view of improving some of this vacant property. I would sell my residence. consisting of eight rooms, with all the necessary outbuildings, such as barn carriage house, corn crib, smoke house, negro quarters, henery, and a beautiful orchard of all sorts of fruit, such as apples, pears, cherries, peaches, plums, grapes, &c. making altogether one of the most comfortable residences in St. Louis county. To persons having children to educate, great inducements are offered in Florissant. They only need to be known to be appreciated. For further particulars apply to S. V. PAPIS & BRO. 33 Chesnut street, or to   MICHAEL POWERS,
   my 6 2m   On the premises.

Newspapers.com

"Some Marks of the Whip on His Back"

Daniel Bissell, a prominent military officer at Fort Bellefontaine, offered a $25 reward in 1817 ($400 today) for the return of **Frederick Sams**, a teenager who had escaped from the Bissell estate called "Franklinville," whom Bissell suspected was in Florissant. As an identifying feature, Bissell notes that the boy's back was scarred from whipping. See illustration, next page.

15 Feb 1817 Missouri Gazette, pg. 1. Newspapers.com

25 DOLLARS REWARD.

Ranaway from Franklinville Farm, on the 23d Inst. a negro boy, called Frederick Sams, born in the state of Georgia : he is about 17 years old, five feet high, short wool, black complexion, knock-kneed, he has a small scar on the forehead, and another on his chin near the lip, and some marks of the whip on his back.—He had on and took with him one Buffaloe robe marked in the centre, Fred. Bissells—one Blanket, an old hat, short brown great coat, blue roundabout with red coller and cuffs which likely he will tear off—three pair of old trowsers, one leather, one brown and one gray twilled kersey, two pair old socks, one blue the other white, a pair of course shoes, red flannel shirt, his apperance is slovenly.

It is expected he is lurking about the neighborhood of Florisant or St. Louis. Whoever will take up said boy and lodge him in St. Louis goal, or deliver him at my farm 8 miles north of St. Lonis, shall receive the above reward and reasonable expences.

DAN'L. BISSELL.

Franklinville Farm Jan. 7.

Opposition to Slavery in St. Ferdinand Township

On June 5, 1819, a group of abolitionists met at the home of Elisha Patterson (1783-1854) to discuss the ongoing debate in the United States Congress over admission of Missouri to the union as a free or slavery state. (Elisha Patterson is the father of Durrett Patterson, a subject of the Winkler essay in Chapter 3 of this book.)

They adopted this resolution calling slavery "contrary" to freedom, a great evil, and (with emphasis) provoking the censure of "a just but *angry* God." The timing was just right. The initial attempt to admit Missouri fell apart in February 1819 after the Tallmadge Amendment (for abolition), and the famous Missouri Compromise that allowed slavery in the state would not be sought until January 1820. Obviously, their effort failed but it showed that there was local opposition to slavery.

FOR THE MISSOURI GAZETTE.

In pursuance of a request, contained in the eighth resolution of a meeting, held in the town of St. Louis, on the 15th day of May, 1819, recommending public meetings, &c. a number of the citizens of the territory of Missouri and county of St. Louis, met at the house of Mr. Elisha Patterson, on the 5th day of June, 1819.

Major Peter Bowler, chosen president, and Mr. Green Dewitt, secretary, both of whom were unanimously chosen.

The following resolutions were then read, and unanimously agreed to.

1. *Resolved,* That we as a free people, view with jealousy any attempt made in Congress to usurp from us, any right with which we may be legally vested by any treaty of cession, or guaranteed to us by the constitution of the United States; but the amendment to the Missouri state bill in the House of Representatives of the Congress of the United States, meets our full approbation, as being more conducive to the present happiness, and future prosperity of this fair and growing country.

2. That slavery is contrary to the term freedom, and it is also contrary to the laws of nature, that one nation, or one individual should be compelled to serve another unjustly.

3. That it is one of the greatest evils we have to regret at this present day in the United States, and if not protested against in this growing country, it will eventually end in an entailed hereditary misery on our future posterity, and bring upon us their just censure, as well as the judgment of a just, but *angry God.*

4. That we recommend to the people of the different counties in this territory, to hold public meetings, and deliberately view this growing evil, and threatening curse of the further admittance of involuntary slavery in the future state of Missouri.

5. That no man, or set of men, shall be censured for his or their opinion or opinions, where every free white man has the right of suffrage.

6. That it be duly considered, that had slavery not hitherto been known, and only introduced at this enlightened age, when we should have been void of its prejudices, and unsullied by a bad education, it would have raised indignation in the mind of every true republican, and the voice of reason have been heard to exclaim, *suffer it not.*

7 That a copy of the foregoing resolutions be transmitted to the editor of the Missouri Gazette, signed by the president and secretary, requesting their publication in his paper.

Done at St. Ferdinand township, this 5th day of June, 1819, in behalf of the meeting.

PETER BOWLER, *Pres't.*
GREEN DEWITT, *Sec'y.*

Missouri Gazette and Public Advertiser, 23 Jun 1819, p. 3.

Of note: Elisha's father was John Patterson, Revolutionary War veteran. It was the **Rev. John Clark Chapter of the Daughters of the American Revolution** that facilitated a major DAR Historic Preservation grant to make needed repairs to Taille de Noyer in 2020. Thank you to the National Society of the Daughters of the American Revolution, and the John Clark Chapter in Florissant. *—Ed.*

The Harris Family and their 1861 Flight from St. Ferdinand Township

The prolific young scholar Cooper Wingert has compiled an outstanding collection of "Stampede Narratives," where enslaved people escaped en masse to free territory. One of the stories he tells is of the Onesimus Harris family's escape from the bondage of the William Patterson, brother of Elisha. The story is part of the National Park Service/Dickinson College "House Divided Project" and can be found online (as of this writing) at: <http://housedivided.dickinson.edu/sites/stampedes/category/escape-narratives/>. The family escaped to Chicago, but due to the Fugitive Slave Act was returned to the Pattersons.

The story has several important dimensions to it. Most notable is the division within the Patterson family over the issue of slavery. As the Winkler essay notes, families truly were divided over the issue and the Patterson family illustrated this.

The Chicago Fugitive Slaves.

SPRINGFIELD, Ill., April 4.—The five fugitives were examined before United States Commissioner Corneau this morning. The proof against them was clear and apparently indisputable. They were accordingly delivered over to their respective owners. The man belonged to Jacob Veale—the women and children to Hiram Patterson of St. Louis county, Missouri. The slaves were taken to St. Louis on the evening train.

The return of Onesimus Harris and his family was covered in the Chicago Tribune, *April 5, 1861. Abolitionists were enraged by their fugitive trial in Springfield, Illinois, and their subsequent return to St. Louis. Jacob Veale was William Patterson's son-in-law. The family escaped to avoid being separated after William Patterson's death in 1860.* Newspapers.com

The First Slavery Code, Louisiana Territory 1804

The first slavery code affecting this area under United States rule was the Louisiana Territory code of 1804. This code would have governed all of Missouri (including Florissant). It provided a law "respecting" slavery (only summary titles shown here) and also made a provision for enslaved persons to sue for their freedom (the opening paragraphs of which are shown on subsequent pages). The code was modified in 1817 after Missouri territory status and again in 1825 after Missouri statehood.

Theising Images

CHAPTER 3.
SLAVES.
CHAPTERS 187, 399.

A LAW entitled a law respecting Slaves.

1. Negroes not to be witnesses except in certain cases.
2. Negroes not to leave home without passes.
3. Slaves not allowed to visit other plantations without passes.
4. Slaves not allowed to carry arms.
5. Free negroes allowed to keep one gun; and more when licensed, and so of slaves.
6. Who deemed mulattoes.
7. Riots among slaves, how punished.
8. Persons not to permit slaves to remain on their plantations, or to meet except in certain cases.
9. White persons found at unlawful meeting of slaves, penalty.
10. Persons found at unlawful meetings of slaves to be apprehended.
11. Persons dealing with slaves without consent of owner, penalty for.
12. Slaves lifting their hands in opposition to white persons, penalty for.
13. Slaves lying out, how to be apprehended.

*See chap. 168, sec. 16, chap. 187 sec. 3.

14. Conspiracy to rebel, or make an insurrection, or commit murder.
15. Administering medicine, penalty for.
16. Slave administering medicine with no evil intent to be acquitted.
17. Slaves administering medicine with consent of owners.
18. Slaves going at large and trading—liability of owner.
19. Slaves permitted to go at large and hire themselves out, to be sold.
20. Twenty-five per centum of sale to be applied to revenue.
21. Selling free persons for slaves, penalty.
22. Stealing slaves, penalty for.
23. Slaves, how emancipated—when to be supported—copy of deed of emancipation to be delivered to negro.
24. Slaves, traveling without copy of deed of emancipation, to be committed to jail.
25. Slave, emancipated, failing to pay taxes, to be hired out.

CHAPTER 35.
FREEDOM.

AN ACT to enable persons held in slavery, to sue for their freedom. *

1. Persons held in slavery to sue as paupers, when.
2. Suits, how instituted—counsel assigned petitioner—petitioner not to be removed.
3. Petitioner about to be removed, defendant

may be required to enter into recognizance; petitioner may be hired out when—person hiring to enter into recognizance.
4. Weight of proof on petitioner—judgment.
5. Appeal to general court.

Be it enacted by the legislature of the Territory of Louisiana, [as follows.]

1. It shall be lawful for any person held in slavery to petition the general court or any court of common pleas, praying that such person may be permitted to sue as a poor person, and stating the grounds on which the claim to freedom is founded. If in the opinion of the court the petition contains sufficient matter to authorize their interference the court shall award the necessary process to bring the cause before them.

2. The court to whom application is thus made, may direct an action of assault and false imprisonment, to be instituted in the name of the person

fore them.

2. The court to whom application is thus made, may direct an action of assault and battery, and false imprisonment, to be instituted in the name of the person claiming freedom against the person who claims the petitioner as a slave, to be conducted as suits of the like nature between other persons. And the court shall assign the petitioner counsel, and if they deem it proper shall make an order directing the defendant or defendants to permit the petitioner to have a reasonable liberty of attending his counsel; and the court when occasion may require it, and that the petitioner shall not be taken nor removed out of the jurisdiction of the courts, nor be subjected to any severity because of his or her application for freedom.

3. If the court, or any judge thereof in vacation shall have reason to believe that the above order has been or is about to be violated, in such case the said court, or any judge thereof in vacation, may require that the person of the petitioner be brought before him or them, by writ of *habeas corpus*, and shall cause the defendant or defendants, his, her, or their agent, to enter into recognizance with sufficient security, conditioned as recited in the above order, or in case of refusal to direct the sheriff of the district to take possession of the petitioner, and hire him

---

*Repealed R. L. 1823, p. 500, sec. 13.

Mathilde's Daughter

by Sister Carolyn Osiek, RSCJ, Archivist
Society of the Sacred Heart

At St. Ferdinand in 1837, there was an enslaved woman, whose name was probably Mathilde. She was there as cook through a lease agreement with another slaveholder. She appears several times in the house journal with her little daughter. She was withdrawn several times, but returned each time. Mother Duchesne lamented that her English was so poor that she could not give religious instruction to mother and daughter. In May 1838, the little daughter died at the age of eight, having made her First Communion before death, and at her funeral, the students in the school carried her coffin to the cemetery.

Public Sales at Florissant

The National Park Service maintains a significant searchable database of the disposition of enslaved people. Some sales were private; many were public sales at the doors of the Old Courthouse in Downtown St. Louis. However, there are three occasions of public sales that were not at the Old Courthouse. One took place at an undesignated place in Bridgeton, but two took place at a "public venue" in Florissant (in 1838 and 1849).

The most prominent piece of public land in Florissant at these times would have been what is now Spanish Land Grant Park—perhaps the only piece of land in Florissant that has never had private ownership.

For more information, see Wilson, Miel, with Bob Wilson. *St. Louis Probate Court Records: Court Ordered Slave Sales.* <https://www.nps.gov/jeff/learn/historyculture/upload/Slave%20Sales%20Database.pdf>

Mary Scott: "Wonderful to be Free"

from Linda Schmerber's
Jennings: The Man, The City, and Its People

In 1844, Mary Scott, age 16, was given as a wedding present to Mary Jane Jennings by her parents on her marriage to Abram G. Switzer. Ragna Switzer Sloane, a descendant, had this story from her family:

> Mary Scott married the coachman and helped raise the Switzer children as well as her own children, [even] after the Civil War. Mary Jane Jennings Switzer's son, Edward, spoke of Mary with respect and affection. She acted as Mary Switzer's right hand in running the affairs of the household [especially after being widowed in 1864].
>
> Mary was supported by Edward, his brothers, and his sons until her death. Edward recalled Mary saying, "Lord, …it was wonderful to be free."

Mary Scott   *Courtesy of L. Schmerber*

Source: Schmerber, Linda. *Jennings: The Man, The City, and Its People*, Jennings Historical Society, 2011. It is available through the Society and accessed through Jennings City Hall.

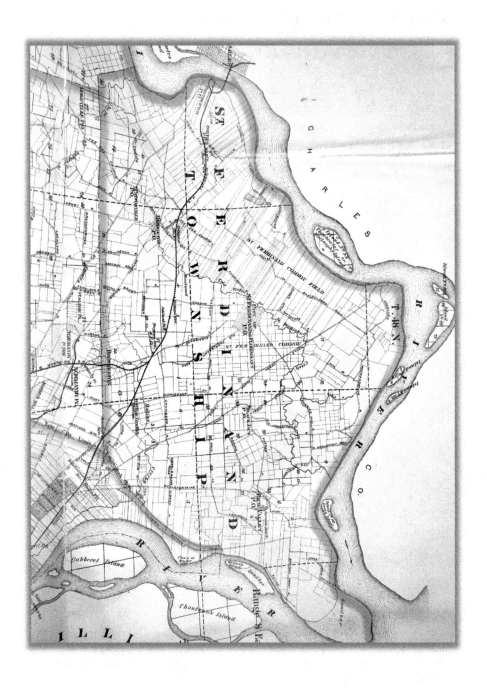

MEDITATIONS

I heard the **singing** of the Mississippi
when Abe Lincoln went down to New
Orleans, and I've seen its **muddy bosom**
turn all **golden** in the sunset.

I've known rivers:
Ancient, dusky rivers.

My soul has grown deep like the rivers.

Langston Hughes, 1921
from The Negro Speaks of Rivers,
inspired by the St. Louis riverfront

FLORISSANT from its very founding has been on the migration route for people from St. Louis. As restrictive laws were repealed throughout the nation, African Americans began a western movement following the exodus of Caucasians. At the beginning of the new millennium Asians and Hispanics were discovering Florissant too.

Some will follow the pattern of their parents or grandparents in moving westward. **Others will stay to meet the challenges that will come and to celebrate a diverse community.**

Visitors still find a place of peace and tranquility in Old Town Florissant. Mourning doves and mockingbirds still greet the dawn, and in the spring iris and peonies still bloom.

Ramon del Valle once said, **"Nothing is as it was, merely as it is remembered."** Florissant remembers and honors its past while building its future.

Rosemary Davison
Florissant, Missouri (2002)

Rosemary Davison (1918-2014) was a humanitarian and one of Florissant's early leaders in historic preservation. This excerpt was from the prologue to her 2002 book on the city.

The Walnut Grove
(an open chain of kwansabas, from the editor)

Beneath the trees, a house to keep.
Around the trees, broad fields to tend.
Under the trees, shade from blazing sun.
What legs rested under those walnut trees?
Which hands (dried, cracked) split the hulls?
Whose child grinned tasting the fallen fruits?
Their names are known only to God.

We cannot make the past go away.
We cannot cleanse truth from the record.
We just may never know the answers.
We can talk and inquire among us.
We can add new ideas to old.
We can shine light on hidden truth.
We can only imagine what they felt.

They were silent; let us give voice.
They were denied; let us say yes.
They had faith; let us be worthy.
They were taken one from the other.
Let us be united to honor them.
They are not here, yet they are.
Their hands made a place for us.

The kwansaba is a poetic form that is seven lines, of seven words, of seven (or fewer) letters. It honors the seven principles of Kwanzaa. It was created 25 years ago by the great Eugene B. Redmond, National Book Award winner and poet laureate of East St. Louis.

I was born in East St. Louis, Illinois, in 1944. Actually because the Catholic hospital in East St. Louis **denied admission to African Americans,** I was actually born in St. Mary's Infirmary in St. Louis – the hospital where the great hero of hope and justice, Sr. Antona Ebo, FSM, worked during those years. I entered the Jesuits in 1962, my family having moved to southern Wisconsin in 1956. When I returned to the area, coming to St. Louis U, for my studies in Philosophy, in 1966, I would visit the novitiate at St. Stanislaus, on several occasions. I did not know any of this history, then.

In October of 1971, a few weeks after I was ordained a deacon as a member of the Society of Jesus, I was invited to assist at a Mass in Kinloch being celebrated by the then-only African American Bishop in the U. S. Catholic Church, The **Most Reverend Harold Perry, SVD.** As we processed out of the church, I asked Bishop Perry if he would be willing to return to the area and preside at my ordination to the priesthood – in East St. Louis, in May of 1972.

My entire life of scholarship has been devoted to remembering and honoring the stories and faith of my family and the people who helped raise me. *In the Walnut Grove* makes my eyes mist up, but my heart to sing. The stories that are told here are essential nourishment for this community. We must tell our stories and **honor the stories** of others, if we are ever to lift the burden of history from our shoulders and walk free and proud and in communion.

Rev. Joseph Brown, S.J., Ph.D.

Father Joseph Brown. S.J., is Professor and past Chair of the Department of Africana Studies, Southern Illinois University Carbondale, and the Founding Chair of the East St. Louis 1917 Centennial Commission and Cultural Initiative. The editor is grateful to Father Brown for his editorial review and assistance in this project (and many others).

The Afterthought

Hear my cry, O God the Reader; vouchsafe that this **my book** fall not still-born into the world wilderness. Let there spring, Gentle One, from out its leaves **vigor of thought** and thoughtful deed to **reap the harvest wonderful**. Let the ears of a guilty people tingle with truth, and seventy millions sigh for the righteousness which exalteth nations, in this drear day when human brotherhood is mockery and a snare. Thus in Thy good time may infinite reason **turn the tangle straight**, and these crooked marks on a fragile leaf be not indeed

THE END.

W. E. B. DuBois
The Souls of Black Folks, 1903

THE FLORISSANT VALLEY HISTORICAL SOCIETY is to be congratulated and commended for its continued efforts in **building on its proud early history.** Bringing the story of early Blacks to light and **the role they played** in the development of the early community is to be commended. Too often Black presence is omitted, overlooked, or ignored. **Building a more diverse story** of the area has the potential of building bridges of understanding that could lead to a better community. This addition also is important to the St. Louis community as it **works toward building a more perfect society.**

Dr. John A. Wright, Sr.
Author, Educator, Administrator, School Superintendent,
Historian of the African American Experience

We boast of the freedom enjoyed by our people above all other peoples. But it is difficult to reconcile that boast with the state of the law, which, practically, puts the brand of servitude and degradation upon a large class of our fellow citizens, our equals before the law. The thin disguise of "equal" accommodations for passengers in railroad coaches **will not mislead anyone,** nor atone for **the wrong this day done....**

from John Marshall Harlan's
dissenting opinion in *Plessy vs. Ferguson* (1896),
the decision that gave us "separate but equal"

We Wear the Mask

We wear the mask that grins and lies,
It hides our cheeks and shades our eyes,
This debt we pay to human guile;
With torn and bleeding hearts we smile,
And mouth with myriad subtleties.

Why should the world be over-wise,
In counting all our tears and sighs?
Nay, let them only see us, while
We wear the mask.

We smile, but, O great Christ, our cries
To thee from tortured souls arise.
We sing, but oh the clay is vile
Beneath our feet, and long the mile;
But let the world dream otherwise,
We wear the mask!

Paul Laurence Dunbar (1872-1906)
Lyrics of Lowly Life, 1896
for whom the elementary school in Kinloch was named

Let us realize that we are **sinners**

and have much to **explate,**

while others, **less culpable** than we are,

suffer more than we do.

St. Rose Philippine Duchesne (1769-1852)

We, the people, declare today that the most evident of truths — that all of us are created equal — is **the star that guides us still**; just as it guided our forebears through Seneca Falls, and Selma, and Stonewall; just as it guided all those men and women, sung and unsung, who left footprints along this great Mall, to hear a preacher say that **we cannot walk alone**; to hear a King proclaim that our individual freedom is inextricably bound to the freedom of every soul on Earth. **It is now our generation's task to carry on what those pioneers began.**

Barack Obama
2009 Inauguration Speech

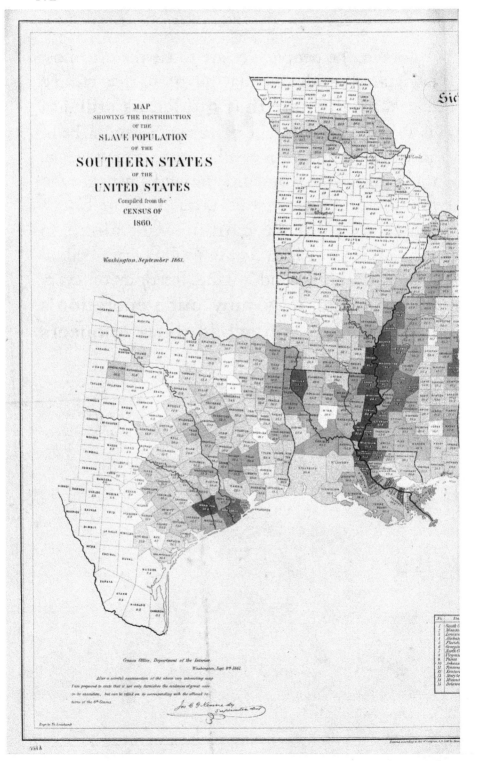

MAP
SHOWING THE DISTRIBUTION
OF THE
SLAVE POPULATION
OF THE
SOUTHERN STATES
OF THE
UNITED STATES
Compiled from the
CENSUS OF
1860.

Washington, September 1861.

Census Office, Department of the Interior,
Washington, Sept. 9th 1861.

After a careful examination of the above very interesting map
I am prepared to state that it not only furnishes the evidence of great care
in its execution, but can be relied on as corresponding with the official re-
turns of the 8th Census.

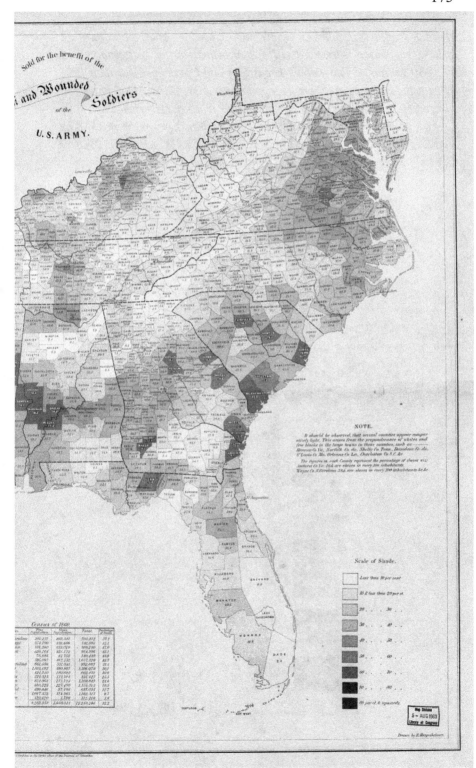

Preceding pages: County-by-county map showing what percentage the enslaved population represented of the total population for that county, from the 1860 Census. Note that St. Louis City and County had less than 10% of the population enslaved, yet the counties north of the Missouri River had more. One can deduce the route of William Walker (Jefferson City to St. Charles, then down the Mississippi to New Orleans), where he would have conducted so much of his business. (See "No Good Masters" in Chapter One.)   Library of Congress

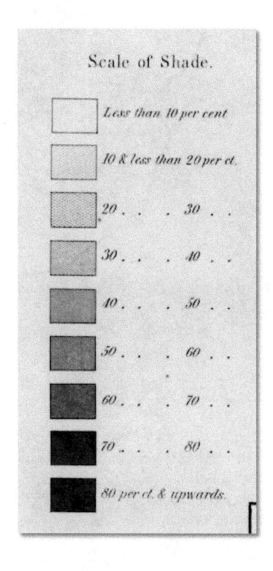

Surname Index

(African American surnames in **bold font**)

Please remember that spellings reflected here may be written phonetically by the census taker or misspelled due to poor handwriting/ transcription errors; if searching for ancestors, consider various spellings of surnames.

9 798561 311390